LONDON RECORD SOCIETY
PUBLICATIONS

VOLUME LV

THE LONDON JUBILEE BOOK
1376–1387

AN EDITION OF TRINITY COLLEGE
CAMBRIDGE MS O.3.11, FOLIOS 133–157

EDITED BY

CAROLINE M. BARRON AND LAURA WRIGHT

LONDON RECORD SOCIETY
THE BOYDELL PRESS
2021 for 2020

First published 2021

A London Record Society publication
Published by The Boydell Press
an imprint of Boydell & Brewer Ltd
PO Box 9, Woodbridge, Suffolk IP12 3DF, UK
and of Boydell & Brewer Inc.
668 Mt Hope Avenue, Rochester, NY 14620–2731, USA
website: www.boydellandbrewer.com

ISBN 978-0-900952-61-6

A CIP catalogue record for this book is available
from the British Library

The publisher has no responsibility for the continued existence or
accuracy of URLs for external or third-party internet websites referred to
in this book, and does not guarantee that any content
on such websites is, or will remain, accurate or appropriate

This publication is printed on acid-free paper

Printed and bound in Great Britain by
TJ Books Limited, Padstow, Cornwall

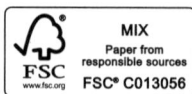

MIX
Paper from
responsible sources
FSC
www.fsc.org FSC® C013056

CONTENTS

LIST OF TABLES

ACKNOWLEDGEMENTS

In the first place we owe a debt of gratitude to the Master and Fellows of Trinity College, Cambridge who have kindly allowed us to publish part of Trinity College Cambridge MS O.3.11 in this edition, and have facilitated our numerous visits to the Wren Library to examine the manuscript. We have received expert help from a number of scholars: Dr. Jane Williams provided information about the Forster family, probable owners of the manuscript in the fifteenth century; Dr. Daniella Gonzalez shared with us her understanding of the 'Common Good' in late fourteenth century English political life and Dr. Adele Sykes Ryan enlarged our understanding of the role played by the common sergeant, Ralph Strode, in the discussions surrounding the creation of the Jubilee Book. Dr. David Moreno Olalla provided expertise on fifteenth-century colophons and textual matters.

We have had exemplary help from the staff at Boydell and Brewer, in particular Emily Champion and Chris Reed (BBR Design).

But we owe a particular debt to Dr. Hannes Kleineke, the Honorary General Editor of the London Record Society who has been a skilful, industrious and scholarly editor and has remained faithful to this project throughout its long gestation. Like the original Jubilee Book, this edition is indeed the result of the 'longe labour of discrete and wyse men [and women]'.

Caroline M. Barron
Laura Wright
July 2021

ABBREVIATIONS

BL   British Library, London

CLBC   *Calendar of Letter-Books of the City of London: Letter-Book C*, ed. R.R. Sharpe (1901)

CLBD   *Calendar of Letter-Books of the City of London: Letter-Book D*, ed. R.R. Sharpe (1902)

CLBF   *Calendar of Letter-Books of the City of London: Letter-Book F*, ed. R.R. Sharpe (1904)

CLBG   *Calendar of Letter-Books of the City of London: Letter-Book G*, ed. R.R. Sharpe (1905)

CLBH   *Calendar of Letter-Books of the City of London: Letter-Book H*, ed. R.R. Sharpe (1907)

CLBI   *Calendar of Letter-Books of the City of London: Letter-Book I*, ed. R.R. Sharpe (1909)

CLBL   *Calendar of Letter-Books of the City of London: Letter-Book L*, ed. R.R. Sharpe (1912)

CPMR 1364–81   *Calendar of Plea and Memoranda Rolls of the City of London, 1364–81*, ed. A.H. Thomas (Cambridge, 1929)

CPMR 1458–82   *Calendar of Plea and Memoranda Rolls of the City of London, 1458–82*, ed. P.E. Jones (Cambridge, 1961)

CPR   *Calendar of the Patent Rolls*

f., ff.   folio, folios

LBH   City of London Letter-Book H (London Metropolitan Archives, COL/AD/01/008)

Liber Albus   *Munimenta Gildhallae Londoniensis: Liber Albus, Liber Custumarum, et Liber Horn.* Vol. I: *Liber Albus*, ed. H.T. Riley (Rolls Series, 1859)

Liber Custumarum   *Munimenta Gildhallae Londoniensis: Liber Albus, Liber Custumarum, et Liber Horn.* Vol. II, pt. i: *Liber Custumarum*, ed. H.T. Riley (Rolls Series, 1860)

LMA   London Metropolitan Archives

ODNB   *Oxford Dictionary of National Biography*

p., pp.   page, pages

PROME   *Parliament Rolls of Medieval England 1275–1504*, ed. Chris Given-Wilson *et al.* (16 vols., Woodbridge, 2005)

TNA   The National Archives, Kew

INTRODUCTION

by Caroline M. Barron

THE MANUSCRIPT

The text printed here is a version of the Jubilee Book or 'new book of ordinances' compiled in London in the last quarter of the 14th century. It is to be found on folios 133–157 of Trinity College, Cambridge, MS O.3.11, a manuscript largely put together in the third quarter of the 15th century. The manuscript was owned at one time by the London lawyer, John Forster (*d*.1488), the son of the London alderman and mayor, Stephen Forster (*d*.1458), and some of the texts may have been supplied to the compiler by John Vale, who was the secretary to another London alderman and mayor, Thomas Cook (*d*.1478).[1] Whoever put together the Trinity manuscript had access to a wide range of London business sources, including material in the city's Letter-Books, copies of royal charters to the city, and useful legal documents and formularies: all materials that would be of use to a man holding office in London. Some of the items are also to be found printed, in 1502, in *Arnold's Chronicle*: another compendium of useful documents for a London citizen.[2] One of the most substantial items (folios 7–26) is a unique English translation of *De moneta* by Nicholas of Oresme (c.1320–82).[3] Almost all the documents in the volume appear in English.[4]

The manuscript, although written in the same hand throughout and, apparently, at the same time, yet clearly divides into two sections: the collection of useful texts (folios 1–122), which is then followed by ten blank folios, and then a second section (folios 133–157), which is the text printed here. This text claims to be the 'new book of the ancient customs and usages in the city of London' which was 'compiled and

---

[1] For a discussion of the scribe of this manuscript, see below, pp. 27–30.

[2] Linne Mooney, *The Index of Middle English Prose, Handlist 11: The Manuscripts in the Library of Trinity College Cambridge* (Cambridge, 1995), pp. 109–14, items [5], [7], [25].

[3] See *The 'De Moneta' of Nicholas Oresme and English Mint Documents*, ed. Charles Johnson (1956).

[4] For a discussion of John Forster and his family, who seem to have been closely associated with this manuscript, see Jane Williams, 'A Late Medieval Family and its Archive: the Forsters of London, c.1440–c.1550' (Univ. of London Ph.D. thesis, 2011), esp. 145–53.

affirmed' in the first year of Richard II, i.e. 1377–8. It is a unique text and would seem to be a version of the volume which was popularly known as the 'Jubilee Book'.

THE MAKING AND UNMAKING OF THE JUBILEE BOOK

On 16 March 1387, during the mayoralty of the fishmonger, Nicholas Exton, at a particularly large meeting of the common council, it was 'agreed and adjudged' that a book (or quire) known as the Jubilee Book should be taken outside the Guildhall and burnt. The reason for this drastic action was that the book had given rise to great controversies, discussions and disputes among the citizens because it contained, it was alleged, 'certain new oaths of the officers of the said city, and certain new ordinances, repugnant to the old and approved customs of the same'.[5] The volume had been popularly known as the Jubilee Book because the decision to establish a committee to revise the city's ordinances and present to the Commonalty 'those that are of benefit to the city and those that are not' was taken on 1 August 1376, i.e. in the Jubilee year of Edward III (January 1376–January 1377).[6] This was a drastic and almost unprecedented action on the part of the city's rulers in 1387. The burning of books, which was to become comparatively common with the advent of popular heresy, was still uncommon in England. The only other book-burning recorded in the city before this date had taken place in 1320 when the ordinances governing the Lorimers' craft, which had been drawn up in 1261, were burnt in Cheapside at the instance of the Saddlers.[7]

The situation in the city of London in the last quarter of the 14th century was particularly turbulent and rent by factions.[8] There were disputes between grocers and drapers struggling to dominate the export trade through Calais; between different groups of drapers fighting over the distributive trade in cloth; between victuallers who wanted to maintain the food monopolies and the other crafts, known as the non-victuallers, who were anxious to open up a free market in food and so bring down costs; and between those, characterised as radicals, who wished to change the way in which the city was governed and those, characterised as conservatives, who resisted the constitutional changes

---

[5]   H.T. Riley, *Memorials of London and London Life in the XIIIth, XIVth and XVth Centuries* (1868), 494; *CLBH*, 303.

[6]   *CLBH*, 41; LMA, COL/AD/01/008 (Letter-Book H) [hereafter LBH], f. 46. On the celebration of Edward's Jubilee, see W.M. Ormrod, '"Fifty Glorious Years": Edward III and the First English Royal Jubilee', *Medieval History*, n.s. i (2002), 13–20.

[7]   *Liber Custumarum*, p. lix.

[8]   For the seminal study of this period, see Ruth Bird, *The Turbulent London of Richard II* (1949).

or, at least, once they were in place and found to be unsatisfactory, struggled to restore the old order.[9] There was no single 'big issue' that caused the turbulence of London in Richard II's reign. 'Parties' such as they were, were evanescent and temporary groupings. There were conflicting economic interests and, perhaps, class interests: masters fought to restrain the wages and opportunities of their workers, while merchants who imported goods from abroad came into conflict with the artisans in London who made similar goods. But underlying these economic rivalries there were also concerns about the way in which the city was governed. Were the mayor and aldermen acting for the common good of all? Were the artisan craftsmen properly represented in the city councils? Were those elected to civic office acting honestly and conscientiously? In the absence of a constitution or written rulebook for the city, how was it possible for citizens to know their rights, or to assess the probity and effectiveness of their rulers?

In the Good Parliament of 1376,[10] which was dissolved on 6 July, three of the city's serving aldermen – Richard Lyons, a vintner, Adam Bury, a skinner, and John Pecche, a fishmonger – were impeached, among others, for lining their own pockets at the expense of the country at large. Bury and Pecche were long-standing aldermen who had also served as mayors, but Lyons was a comparative newcomer and the accusations against him were more specific, namely of having lent money to the Crown at an extortionate rate of interest.[11] The events in the Good Parliament provoked a reaction in the city. The commonalty of the city, speaking through Ralph Strode, the common sergeant (the traditional spokesman for the citizens at large), made a 'grievous complaint' about the behaviour of the mayors and aldermen who, for many years past, 'having disregarded their oath and the needs of the people', had made ordinances for their own private advantage and had granted lands and tenements under the common seal to various individuals without consulting the commonalty.[12] In response to this complaint, the mayor, John Ward, grocer, on the advice of only five aldermen and eight commoners, summoned a great number of men from the 'principal misteries' to come to Guildhall at eight in the morning on Friday 1 August 1376.

This was a momentous meeting, which instituted a number of radical reforming measures.[13] In the first place the impeached aldermen were

---

9   Pamela Nightingale, 'Capitalists, Crafts and Constitutional Change in Late Fourteenth-Century London', *Past and Present*, cxxiv (1989), 3–35.

10   It was the chronicler Thomas Walsingham who related that the Parliament was said to have achieved '*multum bonum*'; see *The St Albans Chronicle*: Vol. I, 1376–94, ed. John Taylor, Wendy Childs and Leslie Watkiss (Oxford, 2003), p. lxxi.

11   For details of the accusations against the London aldermen, see Caroline Barron, *Revolt in London: 11th to 15th June 1381* (1981), 13–14.

12   *CLBH*, 38.

13   Barron, *Revolt in London*, 14–16.

ousted from office and others elected to take their place.[14] Then it was agreed that the common council in future should be composed of men elected by the misteries rather than the wards so that all the crafts, whether artisan or merchant, should be represented. In future, common council was to approve changes to the city's ordinances and nothing was to be done in secret.[15] Further, it was decided to mark the advent of the new order by the addition of a mullet or star to the common seal of the city.[16]

Only a week after the momentous meeting on 1 August, the names of the men chosen by forty-seven misteries for the newly constituted common council were sent into the Guildhall: only the Grocers, Mercers, Drapers, Fishmongers, Goldsmiths, Vintners, Skinners and Tailors sent in six names, all the rest sent four or two names, making 204 in all.[17] The reforming meeting of 1 August 1376 had been remarkable for the range of matters dealt with and for the speed and efficiency with which the proposed reforms were introduced. A full and detailed account of the meeting was written, in French, into the Letter-Book H of the city.[18]

But the work of reforming city government was not completed in August 1376. The 'radicals' were not content simply to reform the common council: they pressed the king to clarify (or perhaps reinterpret) the clause relating to the election of aldermen to be found in Edward II's 'great charter' to the city of 1319. By a new charter, dated 2 November 1376, Edward III unambiguously declared that aldermen were to be elected every year on St Gregory's day (12 March) and could not be re-elected until a further year had elapsed.[19] This reform was aimed at spreading the responsibilities and powers of this office more widely, but the elections tended to foster faction and disorder at the local level and the annual changeover of aldermen prevented the court from pursuing consistent policies and weakened its response to crises such as that posed by the rebels in June 1381.

But those who met on 1 August 1376 had other long-term objectives: a small committee of two aldermen and six commoners was elected

---

[14] *CLBH*, 38–9.
[15] *CLBH*, 39; '*et qe rien ne dust estre ordeigne en muttre par senestre covyne*', LBH, f. 46.
[16] *CLBH*, 36; Riley, *Memorials*, 400.
[17] *CLBH*, 41–4.
[18] *Ibid.*, 38–41.
[19] *CLBH*, 58. The charter of Edward II to the city in 1319 had laid down that new aldermen were to be elected each year on St. Gregory's day, 12 March, but this had not been observed and aldermen, once elected, had tended to serve for life, or until they chose to resign. On 2 November 1376 royal Letters Patent confirmed the annual election of aldermen, *CPR 1374–77*, 387 and see below, p. 101 and n. 39, and a copy of the 1376 Letters Patent was copied into the Jubilee Book, see below, pp. 122–3. The charters are printed in *Historical Charters and Constitutional Documents of the City of London*, ed. Walter de Gray Birch (1887), 46, 65–6.

4

'to survey and examine the ordinances in the Guildhall, and to present to the Commonalty those that are of benefit ("profitables") to the city and those that are not'.[20] The fortunes of this committee can be fitfully traced in the pages of the city's Letter-Book H. In July 1378, two years after the committee had first been set up, the mayor and commonalty elected thirty-eight men to supervise the city's liberties and to act as seemed most expedient.[21] Finally, on Thursday 23 September 1378 a book of ordinances, '*liber de ordinacionibus*', was finally read to a congregation of the common council.[22] Because certain articles in the book seemed '*difficiles*' and in need of '*pleniori declaracione*', a further three aldermen and five commoners were elected to confer with the thirty-six men previously elected in July, and to examine, correct and '*conscribere*' the articles in the book so that there might be unanimous agreement. The Letter-Book records that this was done. And so, two years after Edward III's jubilee year, the Jubilee Book was finally agreed and seems to have been officially known as the *Liber de Ordinacionibus*.

So, from September 1378 the new book of ordinances, having been finally revised, was operative in the city. Then, during the revolt of June 1381, on Friday 14 June some Londoners joined with a brewer, Walter atte Keye from Wood Street, who 'brought fire with him in order to burn the Guildhall and a certain book called "le Jubyle"'. Thwarted in this attempt, the men moved on to the sheriff's counter (office and prison) in Milk Street where they broke open chests 'looking for a book concerning the constitutions of the city of London (called "le jubyle") in order to burn it if it could be found'.[23] This is the first occasion in which the book of revised city ordinances, the *Liber de Ordinacionibus*, is referred to as the 'Jubilee Book', but it is clear that this is the same book on which the various committees had laboured so hard between August 1376 and September 1378.

It is not clear why Walter atte Keye and his allies wanted to destroy the Jubilee Book. What is apparent is that the reforms in civic government which were agreed in the summer of 1376 and which were to some extent enshrined in the Jubilee Book two years later did not usher in a period of harmony in the city. Quite the reverse. The years 1376–81 probably witnessed some of the most turbulent years in London's history. In the spring of 1377 Edward III had to intervene in the government of the city, removing the mayor, Adam Stable, a mercer, and replacing him

---

[20]   *CLBH*, 41, and LBH, f. 46v.
[21]   *CLBH*, 94, and LBH, f. 88v.
[22]   *CLBH*, 99–100 and LBH, f. 92v.
[23]   R.B. Dobson, *The Peasants' Revolt of 1381* (second edition, 1983), 226–8; from TNA, KB27/482, rex rot. 43; see also André Réville, *Le Soulevement des Travailleurs d'Angleterre en 1381* (Paris, 1898), 206. Walter atte Keye is probably to be identified with Walter de Dene, dwelling at the Keye in Wood Street (Cripplegate Ward), who was accused of 'consenting with the men of Kent and Essex', see *CPMR 1364–81*, 290.

with the grocer, Nicholas Brembre.[24] A year later there was serious rioting between goldsmiths and pepperers, and in August 1378 in a fight near Ludgate a fishmonger and his family were attacked by a gang of Londoners led by William Leek, a tailor.[25] The following October, William Maynard, a waxchandler, led a gang that attacked the house of the king's uncle, Thomas of Woodstock, and the next month groups of craftsmen, led by glovers and cordwainers, rioted to such an extent that the king was provoked into sending a writ of enquiry.[26] It is not surprising, therefore, that in June 1381 Londoners were unable to prevent the rebels from Kent and Essex from entering the city: the disorder and confusion in London that summer were the inevitable consequence of the innovations and factions of the years following the momentous changes of 1376.

After the shock of June 1381, there were further attempts to reform the way in which London was governed before it was finally decided to return to the old order.[27] When the draper, John of Northampton, was elected mayor in October 1381, the city was far from harmonious: the fiasco of the city's response to the rebel incursions the previous June had added recrimination and counter-charges to the existing divisions. But it would seem that Northampton tried to make the constitutional changes effective and he took steps to alleviate the difficulties of those who had not been able to profit by the general rise in the standard of living following the population decline after the Black Death. He abolished the monopolies which prevented food (especially fish) from being sold cheaply, and he ensured that there was an adequate supply of small change (£80 was minted into 76,000 farthings at the Tower Mint on his initiative) so that food and other necessities (including offerings in church) could be bought piecemeal by the poor.[28] There was also a crackdown on prostitutes and other forms of 'unchastity', and on those who cheated at dice.[29] Numerous men were condemned to the pillory for cheating and selling goods short weight, and there was a drive to abolish dishonest brokers and usurers.[30] It was a very busy, reformist mayoralty. And it found favour with the king, who 'had heard well' of Northampton and sent a letter on 6 October 1382 to the sheriffs, aldermen and commons of London urging them to re-elect Northampton, who at

---

[24]   *CLBH*, 57, 60.
[25]   *CLBH*, 99; Riley, *Memorials*, 415–17.
[26]   *CLBH*, 104, 111; Riley, *Memorials*, 424, 427–8; *CPMR, 1364–81*, 275–6, 279.
[27]   See Barron, *Revolt in London*, 19–20; *eadem*, 'Richard II and London' in *Richard II: The Art of Kingship*, ed. Anthony Goodman and James Gillespie (Oxford, 1999), 129–54, esp. 133–6, 144–8.
[28]   *CLBH*, 183, 190–1, 192–6.
[29]   *CLBH*, 174–5, 176, 189, including unchaste priests and the like, see *Liber Albus*, 457–60.
[30]   *CLBH*, 181, 184–5, 192, 197–8, 198–9.

first declined to accept the office of mayor for a second term but was at length persuaded to do so.[31]

But in his second mayoralty (1382–3), things began to go wrong. Perhaps Northampton thought he could act more autocratically since he had royal support. Perhaps power went to his head. Perhaps those who opposed his policies, particularly the Fishmongers (led by Nicholas Exton), began to organise themselves in opposition to him.[32] It would seem that Northampton's behaviour became more extreme and when the time came for re-election in October 1383, he found that he had lost the support not only of a large section of the London population but also of the king, who now favoured the grocer Nicholas Brembre. Northampton refused to accept the outcome of the election, organised armed resistance, was tried before the royal council, convicted (largely on the testimony of Thomas Usk), imprisoned and then banished from the city for ten years.[33]

Clearly the constitutional changes of 1376 with their emphasis on craft participation and annual turnover of aldermen had provided the framework in which Northampton could promote his reforming programme. The Jubilee Book which contained the new reformed ordinances and rules for governing the city was seen by some to be the cause of the problems. The brewer Walter atte Keye who in 1381 wanted to destroy the Jubilee Book was probably not the only Londoner who held such views. The new governing structures were seen, by some, to be responsible for the troubles in the city. So Nicholas Brembre, who had been elected mayor in 1383, embarked upon a policy of retrenchment. In January 1384 the elections to the common council were taken away from the crafts or misteries and returned again to the wards, on the grounds that 'matters in common council had been carried more by clamour rather than by reason'.[34] Three months later, during a parliament held at Salisbury, the king agreed that aldermen might be re-elected every year (i.e. an alderman might serve for several consecutive years provided he was re-elected each year).[35] Then on 20 June 1384, Brembre summoned a special meeting of the common council where a committee of forty-two of the 'best and wisest' men of the city was appointed to examine the articles and ordinances contained in the book called 'Jubile' in order to confirm the '*bones et profitables*' ordinances and to '*anuller*' those that were not.[36]

---

31 *CLBH*, 200–1.

32 *CLBH*, 202–5; *CPMR 1364–81*, 36; Riley, *Memorials*, 473–4.

33 John of Northampton was pardoned by the king in 1390 but remained banished from the city. He was restored to full citizenship in 1395, see *CLBH*, 359, 419–20; see Paul Strohm, 'Northampton [Comberton], John (d.1398)', *ODNB*, *sub nomine*.

34 '*plus per clamour quam per reson*', LBH, f. 173; *CLBH*, 227.

35 *CLBH*, 231, CPR *1381–85*, 386; *Liber Custumarum*, 436–7; *PROME*, vi, 378.

36 LBH, f. 176v; *CLBH*, 234–5.

7

On the last day of July 1384, the committee of the '*plus bones gentz sages discretz de la dite citee*'[37] appointed in June presented its preliminary findings to a meeting of common council: they offered a series of new regulations about the way in which meetings of common council were to be held, and the procedures for electing the sheriffs and mayor, in effect revising the procedures laid down in the Jubilee Book. These ordinances were read (*lieux*), heard (*oyez*) and understood (*entenduz*) by the whole common council and the other good men present there and granted and confirmed for the common profit and to be observed for ever.[38] It was clear that the provisions in the Jubilee Book were in the process of being substantially revised.

But the final quietus of the Jubilee Book did not come until three years later in March 1387, during the mayoralty of Brembre's successor, the fishmonger Nicholas Exton. At this meeting it was decided by a very large group of Londoners (so large a group that they had to move from the usual meeting place in the upper chamber at Guildhall into the large hall below) composed of the common council together with 'reputable and more substantial men of the wards', that the book called 'Jubile' should not simply be revised but that it should be burnt because the 'new oaths of the city officers' and the 'new ordinances' which it contained were 'repugnant to the old and approved customs of the city' and had given rise to 'great controversies, dissensions and disputes' among the citizens. And so the Jubilee Book was taken outside by the sheriffs and burnt in Guildhall yard.[39]

But the burning of the Jubilee Book by Mayor Exton, the aldermen, the common council and the 'reputable and more substantial men of the wards' in March 1387 was not accepted without protest. A series of petitions was presented to the Merciless Parliament[40] held in February 1388 by a number of the London crafts complaining about several measures taken by recent mayors of London.[41] The purpose of these petitions, which seem to have been solicited and encouraged by the Appellants, was to provide 'clamour' in order to justify the Appellants' charges against Nicholas Brembre. There are thirteen petitions in all from nineteen different crafts and among these, the Armourers, Mercers, Leathersellers and Whitetawyers, Painters and Cordwainers listed the burning of the Jubilee Book among their complaints. The Mercers asserted that 'the moost profitable poyntes of trewe governaunce of

37 LBH, ff. 176v, 178; *CLBH*, 234, 240.
38 LBH, f. 179; *CLBH*, 238–43.
39 *CLBH*, 303; Riley, *Memorials*, 494–5.
40 This Parliament, which saw the execution of a number of men close to Richard II, was first called the '*parliamentum sine misericordia*' by the chronicler Henry Knighton, see *Knighton's Chronicle 1337–1396*, ed. G.H. Martin (Oxford, 1995), 414.
41 See Wendy Scase, *Literature and Complaint in England 1272–1553* (Oxford, 2007), esp. 65–82.

the Citee, compiled togidre bi longe labour of discrete & wyse men, wyth-out conseille of trewe men, for (so that) thei sholde nought be knowen ne contynued, in the tyme of Nichol Exton Mair, outerliche were brent'.[42] The Cordwainers (leatherworkers) claimed that Exton had been elected mayor simply by the choice of his predecessor Nicholas Brembre, contrary to the customs of the city which were comprised in a book called 'le Jubilee'. In this book, they asserted, there had been written all the good articles pertaining to the good government of the city. Moreover, the aldermen and the good commons of the city had been sworn to uphold and maintain these customs forever, but Nicholas Exton and his accomplices had burnt the book without the consent of the good commons of the city 'to the great destruction and overthrowing (*"anientissement"*) of many good liberties, franchises and customs of the city'.[43]

These petitions complaining about the burning of the Jubilee Book are the last we hear about the book. It was burnt and disappeared from the record. But a copy, perhaps of one of the earlier versions which was revised in the course of composition in the years 1376–8, did survive. It is clear that John Carpenter, when he was compiling his *Liber Albus* in 1419, had access to a copy of the Jubilee Book: his account of the election of sheriffs, for example, and some parts of his account of landlord/tenant relations, are clearly derived from the Jubilee Book, or from a common source no longer extant.[44] One of the members of the 'compiling committees' may have retained earlier versions of the text which finally emerged as the Jubilee Book and it may then have survived in the private archive of a London alderman. It seems to have been in the possession of John Forster, the lawyer son of the fishmonger and mayor, Stephen Forster, in the 1480s.[45] A copy of the oath taken by the mercer Richard Reynold when he was sworn as sheriff at the Guildhall in 1532 has been copied into the manuscript.[46] The manuscript may have passed into his possession but there is nothing to identify him with the Cook or Forster families of an earlier generation.[47] By the late 17th century the manuscript was one of the many volumes acquired by the

---

[42] TNA, SC8/20/997, printed in *A Book of London English 1384–1425*, ed. R.W. Chambers and Marjorie Daunt (Oxford, 1931), 35; *PROME*, vii, 119. For details of this petition, see L.R. Mooney, 'Chaucer's Scribe', *Speculum*, lxxxi (2006), 97–138, esp. 106, n. 37.

[43] TNA, SC8/20/998, printed in *PROME*, vii, 119.

[44] See below, pp. 25–6; William Kellaway, in his meticulous analysis of sources for the contents of the *Liber Albus*, noted that the sources for these passages were 'not traced'; see his 'John Carpenter's Liber Albus', *Guildhall Studies in London History*, iii (1978), 67–84, esp. 75, 79.

[45] See below, pp. 29–30.

[46] Trinity College, Cambridge, MS O.3.11, f. 158.

[47] I am grateful to Dr. Jane Williams for her help in tracking the later history of the manuscript.

scholars Thomas Gale and his son Roger.[48] They were both graduates of Trinity College Cambridge and between them they donated almost the whole collection of their books and manuscripts to their old college. The manuscript which contains the copy of the Jubilee Book is now catalogued as Trinity College MS O.3.11 in the Wren Library.

THE CONTENTS OF THE JUBILEE BOOK

The only known opponent of the Jubilee Book was a brewer, Walter atte Keye, the volume was burnt during the mayoralty of a fishmonger, Nicholas Exton, and the crafts which complained to the Merciless Parliament about the burning of the Jubilee Book were all non-victualling and so, for these reasons, most people have followed Ruth Bird in assuming that 'whatever else [the Jubilee Book] may have contained, [it] certainly included ordinances against victuallers'.[49] But it should be remembered that the Jubilee Book was compiled during the years 1376 to 1378 when the grocers Nicholas Brembre and John Philpot were mayors. Moreover, the various committees set up to compile and revise the Jubilee Book contained men from a selection of crafts: twenty-five grocers and fishmongers and twenty-one mercers and drapers, together with ten other crafts, including butchers and vintners. Table 1 shows the composition of the various Jubilee Book committees appointed during the years 1376–84.

The Table demonstrates that the compiling and revising of the Jubilee Book was not the work of groups either of victuallers or non-victuallers. It was, however, largely the work of the men of the merchant companies (Grocers, Mercers, Fishmongers, Drapers, Goldsmiths, Vintners and Skinners), but there were also a cordwainer, a corder, an embroiderer, a woodmonger and two saddlers involved. Now that we know something about the contents of the Jubilee Book it is clear that it did not contain ordinances against victuallers (or any other particular group in the city).[50] It is, on the other hand, a volume setting out how the city was to be governed, the oaths and duties of civic officers, the procedures in the sheriffs' courts and regulations about landlord/tenant relations. Its contents are not the work of any particular civic faction.

The Jubilee Book is not simply a compilation of items taken from the city's older volumes of records and custumals, although it certainly makes use of decisions recorded in earlier volumes of the city's Letter-Books, especially Letter-Books G and H. The Jubilee Book is innovative

---

48   See David McKitterick, 'Books and Other Collections', in *The Making of the Wren Library*, ed. David McKitterick (Cambridge, 1995), 50–109, at 61–4.
49   Bird, *Turbulent London*, 56.
50   The only indication of a factional element in the Jubilee Book is the inclusion of the text of the short-lived statute of 1382–3 preventing victuallers from holding judicial office in London or other towns in England; see below pp. 123–4.

in that it attempts, for the first time, to provide a constitution for the city and to gather together in one book all the procedures for electing city councils and officers, whether paid, or annually elected. An important intention of the compilation is to make city officers accountable to those who elected or paid them, and the means of achieving this was to be the oath which every city officer took on taking up office (in all, the oaths to be taken by seventeen different officer-holders are copied into the Jubilee Book). Recently, historians have drawn attention to the important part which the swearing of oaths played in the inauguration of officers in English towns in the later medieval period. The oath-taking ceremony was public and, often, the occasion for civic protest.[51] But less attention has been paid to the content of these oaths. In fact, the oath was a form of job-description: it formed the contract between the officer and those who had chosen him. So the Jubilee Book not only set out the ways in which the mayor, sheriffs and aldermen and common councilmen were to be elected, but also the oaths they were to take. Similarly, the oaths of all the salaried city officials ranging from the recorder down to the sheriffs' clerks and sergeants were also set out, in many cases, apparently, recorded for the first time.

So, whatever else it may have been, the Jubilee Book was, without doubt, a book of oaths. A number of civic oaths are, however, also recorded in the city's Letter-Book D, which is largely an early 14th-century volume. Some of these oaths can be dated by their handwriting to the first half of the 14th century: these include the oaths of the mayor, sheriffs, aldermen, chamberlain and the clerks and sergeants of the sheriffs. All these earlier oaths are in French. These early copies of the oaths have, in some cases, been updated, with clauses added to reflect later decisions. No clauses appear to have been deleted. But, confusingly, Letter-Book D continued to be used to record revised or new civic oaths. Some of these were entered on the flyleaves alongside the earlier versions.[52] Further oaths, some twenty-five in all, were copied into blank folios near the centre of the volume later in the 15th century. These later oaths were all in English except the oath of those men who were placed under frankpledge, which was in French.[53] When John Carpenter came to compile the *Liber Albus*, in the early 15th century,

---

[51]   See James Lee, "'Ye shall disturbe now mans right": oath-taking and oath-breaking in late medieval and early modern Bristol', *Urban History*, xxxiv (2007), 27–38; Christian Liddy, *Contesting the City: The Politics of Citizenship in English Towns, 1250–1530* (Oxford, 2017), 112–21.

[52]   There are nineteen 15th-century oaths recorded in the flyleaves, almost all in French, except the oath of the common councilmen which is in Latin and the oaths of the bailiffs of Queenhythe and Billingsgate, and of the yeomen of the sergeants (of the sheriffs), which are in English. The oath of the wardens of the crafts is provided in both French and English, LMA, COL/AD/01/004 (Letter-Book D), ff. A–D; *CLBD*, 1–10.

[53]   *CLBD*, 192–208. Frankpledge was a system under which the people of a district were sworn as sureties for their mutual good behaviour; see *Liber Albus*, 38.

Table 1: Londoners serving on Jubilee Book committees, 1376–84

Name	Craft		COMPILERS		REVISERS
		1 August 1376 (CLBH, 41; LBH, f. 46v.)	16 July 1378 (CLBH, 94; LBH, f. 88v)	23 September 1378 (CLBH, 99; LBH, f. 92v)	20 June 1384 (CLBH, 235; LBH, f. 176v)
Robert Hatfield	Grocer	x			
John Northampton	Draper	x	x		
William Essex	Draper	x			
Richard Northbury	Mercer	x			
William Kelshulle	Fishmonger	x	x		
Geoffrey Cremelford	Grocer	x			x
William Tonge	Vintner	x	x		x
Robert Fraunceys	Goldsmith	x			
John Pyel	Mercer		x	x	
William Walworth	Fishmonger		x	x	x
John Philpot	Grocer		x	x	
Bartholomew Frestlyng	Grocer		x	x	
John Hadle	Grocer		x	x	
John Organ	Mercer		x	x	x
John Warbultone	Mercer		x	x	x
John Boseham	Mercer		x	x	x
John Heylesdone	Mercer		x	x	x

| Name | Craft | COMPILERS | | | REVISERS |
		1 August 1376 (CLBH, 41; LBH, f. 46v)	16 July 1378 (CLBH, 94; LBH, f. 88v)	23 September 1378 (CLBH, 99; LBH, f. 92v)	20 June 1384 (CLBH, 235; LBH, f. 176v)
William Baret	Grocer		x	x	x
John Southam	Fishmonger		x	x	
Adam Karlille	Grocer		x	x	x
Walter Sibille	Fishmonger		x	x	x
John Horne	Fishmonger		x	x	
Thomas Welford	Fishmonger		x	x	x
John Hoo	Grocer		x	x	
John Rote	Skinner		x	x	x
Henry Vannere	Vintner		x	x	x
William More	Vintner		x	x	x
Henry Herbury	Vintner		x	x	x
William Bramptone	Fishmonger		x	x	
William Stachesdene/Staundon	Fishmonger		x	x	x
Thomas Roolf	Skinner		x	x	x
William Culham	Grocer		x	x	
John Hothum	Grocer		x	x	
John Shaddeworthe	Mercer		x	x	x
John Dony	Mercer		x	x	

		COMPILERS			REVISERS
Name	Craft	1 August 1376 (CLBH, 41; LBH, f. 46v.)	16 July 1378 (CLBH, 94; LBH, f. 88v)	23 September 1378 (CLBH, 99; LBH, f. 92v)	20 June 1384 (CLBH, 235; LBH, f. 176v)
Simon Aylesham	Mercer		x	x	
John Coraunt	Goldsmith		x	x	
John Fraunceys	Goldsmith		x	x	x
Thomas Carleton	Embroiderer		x	x	
John Furneux	Grocer/Tailor		x	x	
John Gille	Draper		x	x	
John Bathe	Weaver		x	x	
William Whetelee	Cordwainer		x	x	
John Estone	Mercer			x	
Robert Launde	Goldsmith			x	
Matthew Passelewe	Grocer			x	
William Houghton	Draper			x	
Adam Bamme	Goldsmith				x
William Ancroft	Mercer				x
John Hende	Draper				x
John Wiltshire	Grocer				x
William Cressewyk	Grocer				x
Richard Hatfield	Grocer				x

Name	Craft	COMPILERS			REVISERS
		1 August 1376 (CLBH, 41; LBH, f. 46v.)	*16 July 1378* (CLBH, 94; LBH, f. 88v)	*23 September 1378* (CLBH, 99; LBH, f. 92v)	*20 June 1384* (CLBH, 235; LBH, f. 176v)
Thomas Extone	Goldsmith				x
John Forster	Goldsmith				x
Thomas Girdelere	Corder				x
John Wade	Fishmonger				x
John Colshulle	Vintner				x
William Kyng	Draper				x
Walter Pykenham	Skinner				x
William Pountfret	Skinner				x
Geoffrey Walderne	Draper				x
William Rule	Draper				x
Henry Brounfeld	?Vintner				x
Roger Exeter	Saddler				x
Elias de Weston	Butcher				x
Nicholas Snypstone	Cordwainer				x
William Oliver	Skinner				x
John Pountfret	Saddler				x
William Hawe	Mercer				x
John Asshurst	Woodmonger				x

he also recorded the oaths of eighteen civic officers, all in French.[54]
The wording of the oaths set out in the Jubilee Book can therefore be
compared with earlier versions of the oaths, where they exist, and also
with the later 15th-century versions in *Liber Albus* and Letter-Book D,
and this comparison reveals some of the distinctive preoccupations of
the compilers of the Jubilee Book. They were concerned to abolish the
taking of bribes and to prevent the misuse of the goods and inheritances of orphans. Many office-holders were also required to maintain
'the ordinances in this book', but once the Jubilee Book was burnt such
clauses do not appear in the later versions of the officers' oaths.

The Jubilee Book describes in some detail how business was to be
conducted in the sheriffs' courts and the responsibilities of those who
administered Newgate prison.[55] In fact, eight of the twenty-four folios
of the book deal with matters relating to the sheriffs, their officers and
their courts. There is no attempt to describe how business should be
conducted either in the mayor's court, or in the Husting court. It is
clear that it was the duties of the sheriffs and their officers, and the
procedures in the sheriffs' courts, which were of particular concern
to those who compiled the Jubilee Book. This is not surprising. The
sheriffs' courts were the busiest courts in London, being held as often
as four times a week and dealing with perhaps 1,000 public prosecutions
and 4,000–5,000 personal pleas or civil cases in a single year.[56] Apart
from the public prosecutions, most of the business in the sheriffs' courts
concerned cases of debt and trespass. Many Londoners would, therefore,
have had experience of the ways in which the sergeants and clerks of
that court behaved, and the dishonest practices that often prevailed, and
they wished to make those officers accountable.

The ordering of the information in the Jubilee Book reveals much
about the priorities of those who compiled it. The text opens with an
account of the way in which the common council is to be elected and
the days of its meetings. This is followed by the election and duties of
the mayor, his officers and household, and then the main city officers:
the chamberlain, common sergeant, common clerk and recorder. Only
then does the compiler turn to the duties of the aldermen, the wardmotes
and, finally, the sheriffs. This ordering of material may be compared
with John Carpenter's *Liber Albus* compiled some thirty years later.
Carpenter begins with the mayor (chapters 1–9), then moves on to the
aldermen (chapters 10–12), and only then devotes a single chapter (13)
to the manner of holding a common council. This is followed by the
role of the sheriffs (chapter 14–17) and a further chapter on the duties

---

54 *Liber Albus*, 306–19.
55 For the work of the sheriffs' court, see Penny Tucker, *Law Courts and Lawyers in the
    City of London, 1300–1550* (Cambridge, 2007), 96–9, 122–30; C.M. Barron, *London in
    the Later Middle Ages* (Oxford, 2004), 163–6.
56 Tucker, *Law Courts*, 163.

16

and households of the chamberlain, common sergeant and common clerk (chapter 18). Whereas the Jubilee Book gives primacy of attention and space to the common council, John Carpenter's main concern is the mayor and the aldermen. It is clear, therefore, that one of the main concerns of the compilers of this 'new book of the ancient customs and usages in the city of London' was to define the ways in which the common council was to be elected and the conduct of its meetings and also its role and responsibilities. The Jubilee Book begins by setting out the election of members by the crafts, and then specifies the days on which the council is to meet and how disagreements at meetings are to be resolved. The common council is given the task not only of electing the chamberlain and common sergeant at law but also the common clerk, the common sergeant at arms, the chamber sergeants and, most surprisingly, the recorder. The common council is, moreover, to be consulted when aldermen wish to change wards, and about the punishment of those who commit violent crimes or behave extortionately as keepers of the Newgate prison. Not surprisingly, the common council is also to be consulted about any change to the 'ordinances in this book'.[57]

It had been decided at the 'reforming' meeting of the commonalty held on 1 August 1376 that when civic ordinances were to be introduced or changed, 'nothing ought to be done in secret'.[58] And so, in accordance with this decision, the oath to be taken by common councilmen which was recorded in Letter-Book H in August 1376 and copied into the Jubilee Book has no clause requiring secrecy.[59] However, the injunction to keep secret what was said in common council was reintroduced into the oath in June 1384.[60] This short-lived concern to achieve transparency in the conduct of civic business can be seen also in the absence of any injunction to secrecy in the oaths to be taken by the common sergeant and the undersheriff and the other sheriffs' clerks, although this had been reintroduced into the oaths by the time they were recorded in the 15th century.[61] The compilers of the Jubilee Book were also concerned about bribery and favouritism, and clauses against this are to be found in the oaths of the recorder, the sheriffs and the aldermen. The recorder is further instructed not to deviate from giving impartial justice 'for gifts, favours, promises or for hate', and a subsequent clause in his oath expands on this:

57 See below, p. 90, f. 136v.
58 LBH, ff. 39, 41, and see n. 15 above. The issue of whether discussions in town councils should be secret or public knowledge was a matter of contention in other English towns at this period: see Liddy, *Contesting the City*, 153–61.
59 *CLBH*, 41–2; below, f. 134, p. 84 and n. 4.
60 *CLBH*, 240.
61 '*lour conseille celerez*' in the oaths of the common serjeant, undersheriff and clerks, *Liber Albus*, 310–11, 317–18.

you shall not accept any gifts from any persons, great or small, if you know in your conscience that it has been sent to you to maintain some cause, or to damage or delay someone's right, rather than for love or friendship.[62]

But the injunction to reject bribes was dropped from the later versions of the oaths of the recorder, aldermen and sheriffs.[63]

The compilers of the Jubilee Book were also very concerned about the care of orphans and the safe custody of their inheritances. Clearly the fate of the children of London citizens, and their inheritances, was a complex issue, since so many citizens had died in the plagues of 1348–9 and 1362. It is apparent that those who survived the plagues sometimes seized opportunities for taking possession of the inheritances of underage children whose parents and guardians had died. The common sergeant had always had a particular responsibility to safeguard the rights of orphans and so it is not surprising to find a clause to this effect in his oath, but a similar clause was also added to the oaths to be taken by the mayor, the aldermen, the chamberlain and the recorder, and the clause was retained in the later versions of their oaths.[64] Moreover, the wardmote articles recorded in the Jubilee Book include an injunction to report on anyone concealing the goods of orphans, but this provision is not found either in the earlier wardmote articles of 1370 nor in the later articles as recorded in *Liber Albus*.[65]

Those who compiled the Jubilee Book were aware that there was much in it that was both novel and controversial, and so a clause to maintain the ordinances in the book was added to the oaths to be taken by the mayor, aldermen, sheriffs and the recorder. The recorder's oath was the most specific:

You shall truly safeguard all the articles in all the ordinances in this book, and you shall not agree to any ordinances contrary to these, nor give any judgment contrary to them, without the assent of the common council of the city.[66]

Not surprisingly, none of the later versions of the oaths to be taken by these civic officials included such a clause. Once the Jubilee Book had been burnt, the injunction to maintain its ordinances was redundant.

[62]   See below, p. 101, f. 142v.
[63]   See below, pp. 101–2, 110, ff. 142v, 143v, 147.
[64]   Below, ff. 136v, 140v, 142v, 143.
[65]   *CLBG*, 271–2; *Liber Albus*, 257–60, 332–8; below, p. 107, f. 145v.
[66]   Below, p. 101, f. 142v.

THE DATING OF THIS VERSION OF THE JUBILEE BOOK

There is no entry in Letter-Book H which records the formal acceptance by the common council of the *Liber de Ordinacionibus* or Jubilee Book. But on 16 July 1378 it was recorded that thirty-eight men were elected by the 'mayor and commonalty' to supervise the liberties of the city. Two months later, on 23 September, the *Liber de Ordinacionibus* was read at a meeting of the common council and because some articles were difficult (*difficiles*) and in need of further explanation (*pleniori declaracione indigebant*) the original reviewing committee of thirty-eight was recalled, together with two additional aldermen and four additional common councilmen, to examine, correct and '*conscribere*' the ordinances in the book. This was done and it was recorded that the revisions were agreed unanimously and written into the book.[67] On the same day, William Cheyne, the recorder, complained about the decline in his income brought about by the stipulations in the book of ordinances that the recorder could not receive any fees or robes of a 'foreign lord' while he held civic office. His complaint was referred to the 'reviewing committee', who agreed that the recorder should receive an additional forty marks from the Chamber, over and above the £40 salary laid down in the Jubilee Book, to compensate for this loss of income. This addition to the recorder's salary does not appear in the text printed here.[68] It is clear from other entries recorded in Letter-Book H that the ordinances in the Jubilee Book were, in fact, modified on several occasions before the book was finally burnt. On 9 August 1376 the 'immense commonalty' had agreed that those elected to the common council should be exempt from serving on inquests or juries or as assessors of the tallage. This exemption was confirmed on 7 January 1383, but with an exception added, that members of the common council were, however, to serve on watches with the mayor, sheriffs or alderman of their ward. This exception is not included in the Jubilee Book, which suggests that the compilation predates January 1383.[69] Likewise the oath of the common councilman as agreed at the same meeting on 9 August 1376 is the one to be found in the Jubilee Book rather than the later version of June 1384, which reintroduced the injunction to secrecy.[70] It would appear, therefore, that the text of the Jubilee Book printed here is an early version, to be dated between July and September 1378. It may be a copy of the text which at this point, perhaps, was in the possession of one of the scribes or compilers. The official copy, which would have remained at the Guildhall, and would have been amended as these

---

[67]   *CLBH*, 94, LBH, f. 88v; *CLBH*, 99–100; LBH, f. 92v.
[68]   *CLBH*, 100 and see below, p. 99, f. 142.
[69]   *CLBH*, 44, 209, see below p. 86, f. 135.
[70]   *CLBH*, 41, 240, see below p. 84, f. 134.

later changes were agreed, was the copy which was burnt in Guildhall yard in 1387. But the 'unofficial' copy which was not burnt does seem to have had some later additions, if not amendments or corrections. The copies of charters which appear at the end of the main text may have been added later: certainly the articles regulating the activities of victuallers which were laid down in the Parliament held at Westminster in November 1382 must be a later addition, although as the text now stands all the additional charters appear to be written in the same hand and at the same time.[71]

The text that is printed here is written in English in the 1480s. Dr. Wright discusses the language of the text as we now have it, and the difficult issue of the language of the text, or texts, which the Hammond scribe was copying.[72] That language may have been Latin, Anglo-Norman or English or a mixture of all three. Nothing written in English has survived among the city's records before November 1383 (just after Brembre had been elected mayor and in the aftermath of the rioting at the October mayor's election), when three English proclamations about conventicles, the sale of fish and nightwalking issued by the mayor were copied into the city's Letter-Book.[73] But although the city may have been slow to use English officially (as was also the case with the English royal government, unlike the government in France which was using the vernacular from at least the early 14th century), it is clear from the surviving London returns to the enquiry into guilds in 1388 that the crafts and parish fraternities were drawing up ordinances and oaths in English from a much earlier date.[74] The Carpenters appear to have drawn up ordinances in English as early as 1333, the Pouchmakers in 1356, the Curriers in 1367–8, the guild of the Virgin in St. Stephen Coleman Street in 1369, the guild of St. Anne in St. Lawrence Jewry in 1372 and the Joiners in St. James Garlickhythe in 1375. There were probably many other craft and religious guilds in London using English for their ordinances and oaths whose returns to the 1388 enquiry have not survived. It seems likely that English was a much more utilitarian, administrative language in London in the mid-14th century than the surviving records from the city's Guildhall archive would suggest.

In the Preamble (which has, unfortunately, been damaged) the authors of the Jubilee Book refer to the 'great diligence' and costs of searching in the city's 'various great books' for the 'good articles touching the principal governance of the city'. The purpose of compiling the Jubilee Book was not only to make city officers more accountable, but also to make city government more transparent (hence the removal from

[71]   See below, p. 123, f. 156.
[72]   See below, pp. 30–6.
[73]   *CLBH*, 226; Riley, *Memorials*, 480–2.
[74]   C.M. Barron and Laura Wright, 'The London Middle English Guild Certificates of 1388–9', *Nottingham Medieval Studies*, xxxix (1995), 108–45.

the oath of the common councilmen the injunction to keep secret the business of meetings) and one way of doing this might have been to provide 'the ancient customs and usages of the city' in an accessible language, namely in English. In two places in the Jubilee Book the use of English is specified. When a meeting of the wardmote is summoned, the alderman was to instruct his clerk 'to read aloud in English' the articles of the wardmote.[75] In relation to pleadings in the city's courts, 'All those who bring suits in city courts shall plead in English, and in no other way, so that lay people may know the manner of their pleas'.[76] It had already been agreed in 1356 that pleadings in the sheriffs' courts were to be in English, but the provision in the Jubilee Book extended this to all city courts.[77] If some parts of the Jubilee Book were written in English this may have been one of its most radical aspects and, indeed, may have contributed to the clamour and discord which it was claimed it had provoked. It may have been the form, as much as the content, which made the Jubilee Book so radical.

Moreover, the men who came together to compile the Jubilee Book were not illiterate louts. Many of them knew Latin and French: we know that the London embroiderer, Thomas Carleton, who served on the Jubilee Book compiling committee in July 1378,[78] owned a commonplace book largely written in Latin.[79] There is a comparable compilation in the British Library which was made by, or for, a London fishmonger c.1395, and contains many items copied from the city's records, including an English translation of the charters granted to the city by Richard II in the first and seventh years of his reign.[80] Such men had knowledge of Latin and French but they were also accustomed to using English in the books or ordinances or oaths associated with the crafts and fraternities to which they belonged. If the governing of crafts could be conducted in English, why not that of the city? In this way city government would be made truly accessible and city officers could be brought to account more easily. The use of English enabled the entry of lay people into what Steven Justice has called 'clerkly space'. This caused monks and royal officials to throw up their hands in horror in 1381 and it seems to have provoked a similar reaction in London in 1384–7.[81] When lay people entered 'clerkly space' there were riots, unruly debates, shouting

---

[75]   Below, p. 105, f. 145.
[76]   Below, p. 121, f. 155.
[77]   28 Sept. 1356, *CLBG*, 73. In 1362 the use of English in all law courts had been enjoined by statute, *PROME*, v. 152–3.
[78]   *CLBH*, 94, 100.
[79]   See Hannes Kleineke, 'Carleton's Book: William FitzStephen's "Description of London" in a Late Fourteenth-Century Common-Place Book', *Historical Research*, lxxiv (2001), 117–26.
[80]   BL, Egerton MS 2885, f. 50.
[81]   Steven Justice, *Writing and Rebellion: England in 1381* (Berkeley and Los Angeles, 1994), esp. chapter 1 and 66.

(rather than reason) and a plethora of opinions. In these circumstances it is not hard to see why it seemed better in 1387 to return to the old and safe ways, and to burn the Jubilee Book.

THE COMPILER OR SCRIBE OF THE JUBILEE BOOK

There may have been several scribes at work on the text, and different scribes at different times during the two years when it was being compiled. The common clerk of London at this time was a man named Henry Perot, appointed to the office in August 1375.[82] By March 1381, John Marchaunt (who would succeed Perot as common clerk after 1394) was already in the Guildhall as a chamber clerk, and may have been a clerk elsewhere in the Guildhall before that.[83] The participation of the common clerk, or one of his clerks, in the compiling of the Jubilee Book might be suggested by the detail with which their various remunerations are recorded.[84] But another city civil servant who may well have had a hand in compiling the Jubilee Book is the Oxford scholar Ralph Strode, who was the city's common pleader or common sergeant from October 1373 to December 1382.[85] Strode had begun his career as a fellow of Merton College Oxford in 1359, where he was well regarded as a logician and philosopher, and where he engaged in lively and friendly dispute with John Wyclif.[86] Unexpectedly, perhaps, Strode left Oxford in 1373 and took up the post of London's common sergeant.[87] It seems likely that he moved from Oxford to become a civil servant in London because he was, or wanted to be, married and he could not do this and remain the fellow of a college. Strode was married to a woman named Emma and had a son, Ralph, born at about this time (he was of age when his mother drew up her will in 1394).[88] Two years after Strode

---

[82]   8 Aug. 1375, *CLBH*, 8; 22 Mar. 1374, Perot had previously acted as an attorney in the mayor's court, *CPMR, 1364–81*, 175.

[83]   12 Mar. 1381, *CLBH*, 163.

[84]   Below, pp. 96–7, ff. 140–140v.

[85]   For the duties of the Common Serjeant at Law, see Barron, *London in the Later Middle Ages*, 189–90, 359.

[86]   A.B. Emden, *A Biographical Register of the University of Oxford to A.D. 1500* (3 vols., Oxford, 1957–9), iii, 1807–8, and see J.D. North, 'Strode, Ralph (d.1387)', *ODNB*, *sub nomine*.

[87]   26 Nov. 1373, *CLBG*, 317; 27 Oct. 1375, Strode was granted a mansion over Aldersgate with gardens as long as he held office, and two years later the grant was extended for his lifetime, *CLBH*, 15, 83; 11 Dec. 1382, grant revoked, because Strode had given up office, but 31 July 1384, he was given 4 marks p.a. in lieu of the mansion and two years later this grant was confirmed, *CLBH*, 245, 287; 23 May 1386, Strode appointed standing counsel for the city at a salary of 20 marks p.a., *CLBH*, 288.

[88]   There has been some debate as to whether the Oxford Ralph Strode and the London Common Sergeant Ralph Strode are one and the same man, but '[t]he presumed shift of the same Ralph Strode from the university to a career offering more opportunity for wealth and public advancement, and perhaps also the opportunity to get married,

became the city's common sergeant, and was living in rooms above Aldersgate, Geoffrey Chaucer was appointed to the post of controller of the London customs (1374–86) and occupied rooms above Aldgate. Chaucer at about this time was writing *Troilus and Criseyde*, which he dedicated to 'moral Gower' and 'philosophical Strode'.

The common sergeant was, very specifically, the officer of the commons of the city and conducted prosecutions on their behalf. He was 'their advocate and mouth as the recorder is the mouth of the mayor and aldermen'.[89] It was his duty to present to the mayor and aldermen, or to a congregation of the citizens, petitions, complaints and infringements of the customs of the city. And it was in this capacity that he brought to the attention of the mayor and aldermen the grievous complaints of the commonalty of the city about the self-interested activities of some of the aldermen in July 1376 following the Good Parliament, and thus set in train the various meetings that led to the compilation of the Jubilee Book.[90]

The common sergeant also had a particular responsibility for city orphans, speaking on their behalf, watching over their interests and calling their guardians to account. Ralph Strode seems to have been a particularly active common sergeant. Between his appointment in 1373 and 1382 he appears frequently in the pages of the city's records, on twelve occasions prosecuting cases on behalf of city orphans and on eighteen occasions prosecuting men for food offences, using false measures, bad workmanship, blocking common rights of way or, on one occasion, shooting at pigeons perched on rooftops with bolts and thus endangering men, women and children.[91] Perhaps it was in recognition of his hard work that in October 1375 he was granted a 'mansion' over Aldersgate.[92] In November 1377 he was granted the Aldersgate 'mansion' not simply while he held office, but for life, and this might have been in recognition of his labours in helping to compile the Jubilee Book.

There are some indications in the Jubilee Book itself which might suggest the influence of the common sergeant. There is a marked emphasis throughout the book on the responsibilities of all city officers to guard the rights of orphans (for example, the new clauses that are added to the oaths taken by the mayor, the recorder, the chamberlain and the aldermen), and it was the common sergeant who spoke for orphans

---

is many times more plausible than the existence of two Ralph Strodes, more or less exact contemporaries, of equal eminence': Derek Pearsall, *The Life of Geoffrey Chaucer* (Oxford, 1992), 134.

[89] Betty Masters, 'The Common Serjeant', *Guildhall Miscellany*, ii (1967–8), 379–89, at 380.

[90] *CLBH*, 38.

[91] Information provided by Adele Ryan Sykes in her thesis 'The Medieval Foundations of the Court of Orphans: London and Wardship c. 1250–c.1540' (Univ. of London Ph.D. thesis, 2021), esp. pp. 177–82.

[92] See n. 87 above.

and, as we have seen, Strode appears to have been particularly active in this respect. The text of the common sergeant's oath as recorded for the first time in the Jubilee Book specifies that the common sergeant 'shall preserve and maintain the rights of orphans'. Moreover, in the later, 15th-century versions of the oath the final clause reads 'And attendaunt ye shal be on the mair aldermen and comyns for the causes and nedis of this cite at alle tyme that ye shall be requirid and chargid'.[93] The text of the oath to be found in the Jubilee Book is rather different: 'and the comunes needis of the Citee at al tymes that yee shalbe required bi the Comunes in al placis wher neede shalbe triewly yee shal shewe and tel and ententiefly pursue for the comune profite of the Citee'.[94] The awkward phraseology of this oath may suggest that it was being drafted for the first time, but it is clear that in 1378 the responsibility of the common sergeant was, at that time, solely to the commons of the city and not, as later, also to the mayor and aldermen.

But if Ralph Strode did play an important role in constructing the Jubilee Book, he seems to have lost interest in city affairs. He is last recorded acting as the common sergeant prosecuting on behalf of an orphan in October 1381,[95] and in December 1382 it was noted that he had relinquished his office 'of his own accord' and his Aldersgate 'mansion' was granted to two sergeants of the chamber.[96] The grant of the 'mansion' over the gate of Aldersgate had been made to Strode during the mayoralty of Nicholas Brembre. It was later claimed that during the mayoralty of John of Northampton he had been 'speciously ousted' from the mansion, but when Brembre was once again mayor in July 1384 Strode was given four marks annual rent in lieu of the Aldersgate lodging.[97] Although it is possible that Strode fell out with Northampton, who had been elected mayor in October 1381,[98] it is equally possible that Strode was, in fact, distracted from his civic duties at this time by the various London trials of John Wyclif, which had begun in 1378 and culminated in the condemnation of many of his conclusions at the council held at Blackfriars in May 1382. Strode, who had already engaged in debate with Wyclif at Oxford, may have found combating heresy more exciting than dealing with civic business. Although Strode was no longer active in civic affairs after 1382, in May 1386, when Nicholas Brembre was again mayor, he was retained by the city as

---

93   *CLBD*, 196–7; *Liber Albus*, 310.
94   Below, p. 60, f. 141.
95   *CLBH*, 169.
96   *CLBH*, 208. In June 1382 the Bladesmiths had accused him of betraying their secrets to the Cutlers: *CPMR 1364–81*, 16–17.
97   *CLBH*, 83, 245.
98   There is some suggestion that Northampton may have shared some of Wyclif's opinions and, in this case, he and Strode would not have had an easy partnership: Bird, *Turbulent London*, 62–3.

'standing counsel', at the large annual salary of twenty marks.[99] It is clear that some Londoners valued him highly. But Strode did not enjoy his large salary for long. He appears to have died in 1387: his will was enrolled in the Archdeaconry court, but the copy has not survived.[100] His widow, Emma, continued to live in the parish of St. Anne on the south side of Aldersgate and when she died in 1394 she asked to be buried in the church or cemetery there. She appointed her son, Ralph, as one of her executors together with Margery, the wife of the mercer, Thomas Lucas.[101] If, indeed, Ralph Strode did play a significant role in the construction of the Jubilee Book, it is possible that the Londoners delayed its destruction until after his death.

THE END OF THE JUBILEE BOOK?

The copy of the Jubilee Book which was burnt on 16 March 1387 will have been the most formal copy which was kept and used in the chamber of the city. This would have been the volume which was amended on different occasions between 1378 and 1387. The unusual decision to burn the volume in a public display symbolised the overturning of a policy, the return to the old ways of doing things and to the old ways of governing the city. The turbulence in London did not die down until Richard II took the city into his own hands in 1392 and fined the city the large sum of £10,000.[102] In 1394 the aldermen were once again elected for life;[103] the fate of city orphans and their inheritances were brought under the oversight of the chamberlain and the opportunism of the merchants of the 14th century gave way to a greater concern for the common good.[104] It would seem that an early draft of the Jubilee Book must have remained either in the city chamber or in a private household. In compiling his own 'repertory', the *Liber Albus*, John Carpenter made use of a large number of the volumes then accessible in the city chamber. He often records his sources and William Kellaway, in an article published in 1978, assiduously traced the volumes that Carpenter had used.[105] But he could find no sources for the folios that Carpenter seems to have taken from the Jubilee Book. These relate to

---

99 *CLBH*, 288.

100 *Testamentary records in the Archdeaconry Court of London*, ed. Marc Fitch (British Record Society, 1979), 362.

101 The will was drawn up at Easter 1394: LMA, DL/C/B/004/MS09171, ff. 312–313. In Jan. 1394 Thomas and Margery Lucas had the orphan, Petronilla Oxwyk, as an apprentice; see *CLBH*, 405.

102 C.M. Barron, 'The Quarrel of Richard II with London, 1392–7' in *Medieval London: Collected Papers of Caroline M. Barron*, ed. Martha Carlin and J.T. Rosenthal (Kalamazoo, 2017), 27–55.

103 *CLBH*, 409–10.

104 Barron, *Later Medieval London*, 306–7.

105 Kellaway, 'Liber Albus', 67–84.

city officers and their fees, to the conduct of the sheriffs and their officers and to the relations between landlords and tenants. Carpenter divides up the texts he copies and uses them in a different order in the *Liber Albus*. In John Carpenter's Repertory the texts from the Jubilee Book are all in Anglo-Norman in spite of the fact that English was becoming increasingly the language of government. But Carpenter, together with his friend and patron the mayor Richard Whittington, did not want a repetition of the turbulence that had plagued London in the 1380s. So they played safe and wrote the new blueprint for civic government in Latin and Anglo-Norman.

The fate of the Jubilee Book demonstrates both the power, and the vulnerability, of a written text: its vulnerability is seen in the need to require civic officers (mayor, alderman, sheriffs and recorder) to swear to 'be attentive to all the ordinances in this book, in all their articles, and to uphold them as far as you can, and not to agree to any ordinances or judgements contrary to them without the consent of the common council of the city'.[106] But the extraordinary power of the written text is to be seen in the fact that it seemed necessary in 1387 for the Jubilee Book to be publicly destroyed and burnt.

   This attempt to make civic government accountable, transparent and consultative was not forgotten but lived on in the consciousness of London citizens. Ralph Holland and the London radicals of the 1430s and 1440s demonstrated quite a sophisticated grasp of the way in which city government worked, or could work, in the interests of all its citizens.[107] Perhaps the ideas and concerns that had provoked the Jubilee Book remained alive among the Londoners and shaped their demand for changes in the way in which the city was governed. The focus on the economic rivalries in London in the 1370s and 1380s has failed to take account of the underlying consensus, across the different crafts, which attempted to produce a blueprint for a more broadly based and transparent set of rules for governing the city. The contents of this surviving early version of the Jubilee Book substantiate the claims put forward by the 'folk of the Mercerye' to Parliament in 1388: the Jubilee Book was indeed the result of the 'longe labour of discrete & wyse men' who in the 1370s attempted to compile for London a book which should contain 'the moost profitable poyntes of trewe governaunce of the Citee'.[108]

---

[106]   Below, p. 90, f. 136v.
[107]   C.M. Barron, 'Ralph Holland and the London Radicals, 1438–1444' in *The Medieval Town: A Reader in English Urban History 1200–1540*, ed. Richard Holt and Gervase Rosser (1990), 160–83, repr. in *Medieval London*, ed. Carlin and Rosenthal, 335–60.
[108]   *London English*, ed. Chambers and Daunt, 35.

ON THE LANGUAGE OF FOLIOS 133–157 OF TRINITY COLLEGE CAMBRIDGE MS O.3.11

by Laura Wright

ABOUT THE MANUSCRIPT, PAPER-STOCKS AND SCRIBE

Trinity College Cambridge MS O.3.11 is a late 15th-century paper manuscript book entitled *Customs of London*, which contains copies of statutes, laws and customs, and a translation of Nicholas de Oresme's *De Moneta*. The main hand is that of the scribe known as the Hammond scribe, named after the scholar Eleanor Hammond, who was the first to identify this scribe's handwriting across various texts. To date, fifteen literary, legal, medical, civic, heraldic, religious, astronomical and mathematical manuscripts have been identified as copied by the Hammond scribe, written in Medieval Latin, Anglo-Norman French and Middle English. In terms of size and page-layout, Trinity College Cambridge MS O.3.11 forms a companion to Trinity College Cambridge MS R.14.52, another 15th-century book copied by the Hammond scribe. Both books have the same kind of red, paler red and blue initial decorations, the same red and purple line-ruling, and similar pricking. They also share the same paper-stocks: folio i of O.3.11 and folios 173b and 173d of R.14.52 depict an image of a small church, a seemingly unusual watermark, found (so far) in four books published between 1481 and 1485, giving a *terminus ante quem* of 1485. Someone, then, hired the Hammond scribe to copy legal and civic texts into O.3.11, and scientific and medical texts into R.14.52, and it has been speculated that this someone might have been either Sir Thomas Cook, mayor of London 1462–3, or John Vale, his secretary, whose personal device appears on folio i of R.14.52 and two other manuscripts copied by the Hammond scribe.[1]

---

[1] Vale's device also occurs on f. 170 of BL, Harley 2251 (listed as f. 175 (old-style pagination), by Päivi Pahta, 'Description of the Manuscript', in *Sex, Aging, & Death in a Medieval Medical Compendium. Trinity College Cambridge MS R.14.52, Its Texts, Language, and Scribe*, ed. M.T. Tavormina (2 vols., Tempe: Arizona, 2006), i,

It is not known with any certainty who the Hammond scribe was. Sutton and Visser-Fuchs identify the Hammond scribe as John Multon, a stationer who worked in Paternoster Row,[2] and Pahta refers to Hammond as 'the hand associated with Multon' and 'the Multon scriptorium'.[3] This identification has been made because R.14.52 has inscriptions which read:

f. 215   Quod Multon. 1458.
f. 217   Quod Multon.
f. 219   Quod Multon.
f. 222   Quod Multon.

The preceding texts are in English but there is a change of script for 'Quod Multon'. Parkes says, 'Some scribes signed their copies with the formula "quod" + surname', which is why he has been identified as the Hammond scribe,[4] but Mooney says *quod* 'usually indicates not an owner but an author, translator, or scribe'.[5] Since the name 'Multon' occurs only in one text, a tract about a quadrant, she infers that 'Quod Multon' points to the translator of the quadrant text rather than the name

---

1–17, p. 3, and L.R. Mooney, 'The Scribe', *ibid.*, 55–63, p. 57, but as f. 170 (modern pagination) by A.F. Sutton and Livia Visser-Fuchs, 'The Provenance of the Manuscript: The Lives and Archive of Sir Thomas Cook and His Man of Affairs, John Vale', in *The Politics of Fifteenth-Century England: John Vale's Book*, ed. M.L. Kekewich *et al.* (Far Thrupp, 1995), 73–123, p. 109); and on f. 169v of Worcester Cathedral F.172 (Päivi Pahta, *Medieval Embryology in the Vernacular: the Case of* De Spermate (Helsinki: Mémoires de la Société Néophilologique de Helsinki, liii, 1998), 124). *Sex, Aging, & Death*, ed. Tavormina, is an edition of the companion volume, Trinity College Cambridge MS R.14.52, which Mooney, 'The Scribe', 55–6, dates to between 1458 and c.1485. For John Vale's ownership of Trinity College Cambridge MS O.3.11, see Sutton and Visser-Fuchs, 'Provenance of the Manuscript', 108–9. For a description of O.3.11, see L.R. Mooney, *The Index of Middle English Prose. Handlist XI: Trinity College, Cambridge* (Cambridge, 1995), 109–14. For a discussion of watermarks in O.3.11, and a fuller language analysis of negation in O.3.11, see Laura Wright, 'The Hammond scribe: his dialect, his paper, and folios 133–155 of Trinity College Cambridge MS O.3.11', in *Communicative Spaces: Variation, Contact, and Change*, ed. Claudia Lange, Beatrix Weber and Göran Wolf (Frankfurt am Main, 2012), 227–58.

2   Sutton and Visser-Fuchs, 'Provenance of the Manuscript', 108.

3   Pahta, *Medieval Embryology*, 123–7. Robert Multon, Stationer, rented a tenement in Paternoster Row 1473–95: LMA, CLA/007/FN/02/003 (Bridgemasters' Annual Accounts and Rental, Vol. 3, 1460x1484), ff. 219, 235, 250, 265, 279, 293, 309 and CLA/007/FN/02/004 (Bridgemasters' Accounts, Vol. 4), ff. 3, 22, 40v, 62, 85, 98, 111, 144 and 166v, with a gap in 1480. Pahta, *Medieval Embryology*, 144, n. 13 notes that a Robert Multon was brother to a John Multon, and a Robert Multon was nephew to a John Multon, and suggests that the Paternoster Row tenement was first held by the brother and later by the nephew.

4   M.B. Parkes, *Their Hands before our Eyes: a Closer Look at Scribes: the Lyall Lectures delivered in the University of Oxford 1999* (Aldershot, 2008), 43.

5   Mooney, 'The Scribe', 57.

of the scribe.[6] Reynhout's survey of colophons shows that *quod* was popular with English 15th-century scribes, and that the following name could be that of the main scribe, a commissioner, owner or reader, so 'Quod Multon' remains inconclusive.[7] On folio 178, a blank leaf at the end of O.3.11, there is a copy of a deposition by John Forster, draper, concerning the release by Dame Agnes Forster of Thomas Holbeche, so that he could return home to the manor of Mullesworth. John Forster was son-in-law to Sir Thomas Cook.[8]

[6] L.R. Mooney, 'A Middle English Text on the Seven Liberal Arts', *Speculum*, lxviii (1993), 1027–52 (repr. in *Sex, Aging, & Death*, ed. Tavormina, 701–36), 1028 and n. 8. John Multon, stationer, has been identified as the relevant Multon because a John Multon bequeathed a Psalter to John Vale in his will (Sutton and Visser-Fuchs, 'Provenance of the Manuscript', 108; Pahta, *Medieval Embryology*, 124), but Mooney, 'The Scribe', 59, also suggests William Multon, Bordeaux Herald, who may have worked at the King's Wardrobe, because one of the texts copied by the Hammond scribe, BL, Add. MS 29901, is to do with heraldry (L.R. Mooney, 'A New Manuscript by the Hammond Scribe, Discovered by Jeremy Griffiths', in *The English Medieval Book: Studies in Memory of Jeremy Griffiths*, ed. A.S.G. Edwards, Vincent Gillespie and Ralph Hanna (2000), 113–23). Estelle Stubbs, 'Clare Priory, the London Austin Friars and Manuscripts of Chaucer's Canterbury Tales' in *Middle English Poetry: Texts and Traditions: Essays in Honour of Derek Pearsall*, ed. A.J. Minnis (York, 2001), 21–2 suggests Friar John Multon of Clare Priory, and there were also further possible John Multons, such as the London hosteller who occurs in 1471 in Plea and Memoranda Roll A 91, m. 5v (*CPMR 1458–82*, 166) and John Multon, yeoman of Southwark, whose will was proved 14 November 1508 (TNA, PROB11/16, f. 63v).

[7] Lucien Reynhout, *Formules Latines de Colophons* (2 vols., Turnhout, 2006), i, 196.

[8] A.I. Doyle, 'An Unrecognized Piece of Piers the Ploughman's Creed and Other Work by its Scribe', *Speculum*, xxxiv (1959), 428–36, p. 430, n. 16; Pahta, *Medieval Embryology*, 123–4. Holbeach and Moulton are two neighbouring villages in Lincolnshire (although both Holbeach and Moulton repeat as toponyms elsewhere in England). It may be coincidence that the name 'Thomas Holbeche' occurs on f. 178 of O.3.11, and the name 'Multon' in R.14.52, the sister volume which shares the church watermark, or, Thomas Holbeche and Multon may have been one and the same person. Thomas de Multon was Lord of Holbeach in 1252, for example, and there were others similarly named from around 1100 until that line died out in 1336 (Thomas Allen, *The History of the County of Lincoln from the Earliest Period to the Present Time* (1833), 334). The Thomas Holbeche mentioned in the deposition was chief assistant to John Forster, receiver-general to Queen Elizabeth Woodville (A.R. Myers, 'The household of Queen Elizabeth Woodville, 1466–7', *Bulletin of the John Rylands Library*, l (1967), 207–35, 443–81, p. 213). This Holbeche was clerk of the Receipt, and he compiled John Forster's household account book for the queen for the years 1466–7 (TNA, E36/207). Folio 24 reads: "*Et solut⁹ Thome holbache Clĩco Re^{te} Regine scribn istum librũ*", 'and paid to Thomas Holbache Queen's Clerk of the Receipt for writing this book'. If this Thomas Holbeche and 'Multon' were one and the same person, then Multon is not the Hammond scribe. The <W> of Holbeche's account, TNA, E36/207, is curly, the <v> has an initial loop, the <h> descender wiggles, <B> has a diagonal NE–SW ascender. The Hammond scribe's script is less curly, the descenders less loopy, and Hammond's long <s> ascenders are distinctive.

Summing up the *dramatis personae* linked to O.3.11:

a) the scribe who copied the text in the second half of the 15th century, named after scholar Eleanor Hammond

b) Multon, which name appears four times in a text about a quadrant in O.3.11's companion volume R.14.52 and so has been identified by some as the Hammond scribe although others disagree; a John Multon bequeathed a psalter to John Vale

c) John Forster, son-in-law to Sir Thomas Cook, receiver general to Queen Elizabeth Woodville, deponent on blank leaf at end of O.3.11

d) Dame Agnes Forster I, widow of Stephen Forster, mayor 1454, mother of John Forster, named in a deposition on a blank leaf at the end of O.3.11

e) Thomas Holbeche, Clerk of the Receipt to Queen Elizabeth Woodville and assistant to John Forster, named in a deposition on a blank leaf at the end of O.3.11

f) Robert Morton, gentleman, husband of Agnes Forster II, who was the daughter of Agnes I and Stephen Forster, and hence brother-in-law to John Forster, named in deposition on blank leaf at end of O.3.11. This Robert Morton and Agnes II had a son, (another) Robert, who became heir to his uncle John Forster when the latter died in 1488[9]

g) John Vale, secretary to Sir Thomas Cook, whose personal device occurs in R.14.52 and two other manuscripts by the Hammond scribe

h) Sir Thomas Cook, mayor 1462–3 and father-in-law of John Forster, employer of John Vale, thereby circumstantially linked to O.3.11 and possibly its commissioner

ABOUT THE LANGUAGE

The spellings in the Jubilee Book (that is, folios 133–155 of O.3.11, omitting the charters on folios 155–7) reflect the Hammond scribe's usual spelling practices, meaning that they are of late 15th-century date and tell us nothing about the 14th-century original.[10] The Hammond scribe's notable spelling practices include:

9   M.P. Davies, 'Stephen Forster', in *The History of Parliament: The Commons 1422–61*, ed. Linda Clark (7 vols., Cambridge, 2020), iv, 425–30, p. 429.

10 For the Hammond scribe's own dialect, see the summary in Wright, 'Hammond scribe'; for a description of the Hammond scribe's spelling and letter-graph practices in Worcester F.172, ff. 138r–146v, particularly with regard to his distinctive use of <ie>, see Vincent Dimarco and Leslie Perelman, *The Middle English Letter of Alexander to Aristotle* (Amsterdam, 1978).

<ie> digraphs: e.g. *bien* 'been', *thiese* 'these', *triew* 'true'
<uy> digraphs: e.g. *fuyre* 'fire', *shuyres* 'shires', *toguyder* 'together'
–n on plural verbs: e.g. *wiln, wern, shuln, mown*
singular/plural distinction: *shal/shuln*
variable use of <g> as opposed to <y>: e.g. *guyldhalle, ageyn*

These spellings are found in O.3.11 and all his other English writings. It has been argued that they constitute regional spellings from Essex/ Suffolk or Kent respectively.[11] Both localisations are plausible, but these rather few personal spelling habits do not necessarily place the Hammond scribe outside London, as written London English of the late 15th century encompassed a wide range of variation.

ON ENGLISH NEGATOR PARTICLE *NE*

At what date was the Hammond scribe's exemplar composed, and in what language? Folio 133 of O.3.11 states 'compiled and affermed bi the Maire Aldermen and Comunes of the same Citee the yeer of kyng Richard the secunde the first yeer'; giving a *terminus post quem* of 1377–8, and on folio 155v there appears a statute which was repealed when Nicholas Brembre was mayor, giving a *terminus ante quem* of between September 1382 and November 1383. Thus on internal dating, the Jubilee Book was compiled in the six years between 1377 and 1383. But was the Hammond scribe's exemplar also in English of this date? There are two references in the text to the official speaking of English: 'And the Alderman ought to make his Clerk openly to Rede in Inglissh the poyntes that ensuen' (O.3.11, f. 145); 'also that al pleaters that pleaten withyn the Citee shuln pleate in Inglissh and in nonother man(er) so that the lay people mown knowe the man(er) of (their) plees' (O.3.11, f. 154v). *Lay* in this context means 'uneducated', the inference being that non-professional Londoners of the late 1370s did not understand Medieval Latin and Anglo-Norman French.[12] The first injunction suggests that the 'poyntes that ensuen' were composed in the English language, so

[11] L.M. Matheson, 'The Dialect of the Hammond Scribe', in *Sex, Aging, & Death*, ed. Tavormina, i, 65–93; Simon Horobin, 'Linguistic Features of the Hammond scribe', *Poetica*, li (1999), 1–10.

[12] *Middle English Dictionary* lai (adj.) (a) 'unlearned, uneducated'. In a series of articles, Ingham has shown that Anglo-Norman was used as a spoken language by professionals until the end of the 14th century, after which it was abandoned, and these two comments in the Jubilee Book corroborate his observation (Richard Ingham, 'Mixing languages on the manor', *Medium Ævum*, lxxviii (1) (2009), 80–97; *idem*, 'Code-switching in the later medieval English lay subsidy rolls' in *Code-Switching in Early English*, ed. Herbert Schendl and Laura Wright (Berlin, 2011), 95–114; *idem*, 'Language-mixing in medieval Latin documents: vernacular articles and nouns' in *Multilingualism in Medieval Britain 1100–1500: Sources and analysis*, ed. J.A. Jefferson and Ad Putter (Turnhout, 2012), 105–22; see Laura Wright, 'On variation and change in London medieval mixed-language business documents' in *Language Contact and Development around the*

we compared the text on O.3.11, folios 133–155 (omitting the charters on folios 155–157) with the Hammond scribe's other writing in English, and other London English writing of the late 14th century. We found that the language of O.3.11 is not unlike the Hammond scribe's other writing in English, with one exception: there is an unusually high frequency of the particle *ne* negating tensed verbs in some, but not all, of O.3.11's texts.

By the late 15th century, *ne* was no longer customary when forming negatives; indeed, it was becoming abandoned in texts written one hundred years earlier. That is, texts of the late 14th century show some verbs negated with *ne* and some without, whereas pre-14th-century texts always show *ne* and post-15th-century ones never do. By the late 15th century there was no need for the Hammond scribe to include negative particle *ne* at all in O.3.11, and it must have appeared old-fashioned at the time.[13] The companion volume, R.14.52, which is also made up of composite texts, has just 4% *ne* usage, whereas folios 133–155 of O.3.11 have 42% negative-tensed verbs preceded by *ne*. Table 3 in the Appendix shows a breakdown of whereabouts in O.3.11 the negative particle *ne* on tensed verbs occurs.

Folios without instances or runs of *ne* followed by a tensed verb are: 1–67, 69–70, 71–73, 74–86v, 102–115v; that is, most of the manuscript. All the tensed verbs preceded by *ne* on folios preceding folios 133–155 are in texts known to have been composed in the 14th century. A further comparison between folios 133–155 of O.3.11 and fourteen London English late 14th-century texts of similar subject matter reveals a similar pattern: five have no negative particle *ne* at all, and nine have variable ratios, like our Jubilee text.[14] The Hammond scribe could have avoided *ne* altogether as he did elsewhere, had he chosen to fully modernise his exemplar, but instead he retained this feature when copying 14th-century texts. We therefore conclude that the original text of O.3.11, folios 133–155, was likely to have been composed in English in the 14th century, and indeed was not originally composed in the later 15th century when the Hammond scribe copied it.

ON ANGLO-NORMAN NEGATOR PARTICLE *NE*

The text of folios 133–155 is not homogenous; it is made up of separate job descriptions (oaths), procedural processes, and details of how the city of London was to be governed. Some of these passages are known to have been in existence in Richard II's reign, which, if it is indeed the Jubilee

---

North Sea, ed. Merja Stenroos, Martti Mäkinen and Inge Særheim (Amsterdam and Philadelphia, 2012), 99–115, pp. 111–13 for a synopsis).

[13]   As in *he ne hath* 'he does not have' (f. 150v), or *ne brewe nat* 'do not brew' (f. 150). *Ne* could also act as a conjunction: *ne … ne* 'neither … nor'. Conjunction *ne* has been excluded from the count.

[14]   Wright, 'Hammond scribe', 234.

text, is when it would have been drafted. The oaths of the mayor, aldermen, recorder, sheriffs, constables, scavagers, beadles, chamberlain, common sergeant of law, common sergeant of arms, common clerk, sergeants of the mayor and chamber, those put in freepledge, under sheriffs and their clerks, sheriff's sergeants and sergeants' yeomen, are English translations, often word for word, of the oaths written in Anglo-Norman in the City of London Letter-Book D, and also copied into the City of London custumal *Liber Albus* (in terms of dating, the oaths on folios D verso and I recto of Letter-Book D are written in 14th-century hands and are likely to precede the Jubilee Book copies; the rest of the oaths in Letter-Book D and *Liber Albus* were written after the Jubilee Book versions).[15] Doyle says of another manuscript written by the Hammond scribe:

> The selection of works in Worcester F.172, especially the papal, provincial, and diocesan statutes, notes on the office of a bishop or priest, on the right to tithes and the power of excommunication, and regulations for series of masses, as also certain parallel Latin texts or cues, and liturgical annotations added as late as the sixteenth century, suggest a strongly sacerdotal interest. Yet the very putting of such items into the vernacular is exceptional, and these are for the most part not only unique copies but also unique renderings, done so literally as to depend on the originals for intelligibility, that is, rather as cribs for consultation than for independent circulation.[16]

Two things stand out: 1) that use of English is exceptional, 2) that the translation is literal and done as a 'crib for consultation'. The Hammond scribe's unusual *modus operandi* was to 'uniquely render' certain legal or administrative Latin and French texts into a kind of virtual English (or to copy out such translations, if the translations were not his own). This raises the question of whether the Hammond scribe was copying a text which was originally written in English, or whether he was copying a translation from an exemplar written in Anglo-Norman French. We observe that the Jubilee Book text is different from the 15th-century texts in O.3.11 because the Hammond scribe did not update the old-fashioned *ne*s therein. The fact that the Jubilee Book portion is different with regard to *ne* usage from the other (15th-century) portions of O.3.11 makes it likely that the exemplar or exemplars were written in the 14th century, but we cannot automatically assume that the underlying text was written in 14th-century English because the Hammond scribe may have translated from Anglo-Norman originals, keeping many of the Anglo-Norman word-stems and the underlying Latinate word order, and keeping also the Anglo-Norman negative *ne* particles – as both English and

15 LMA, COL/CS/01/012 (*Liber Albus*), ff. 207v–211, printed in *Liber Albus*, 306–19; COL/AD/01/004 (Letter-Book D) flyleaves – ff. 1r, lxxxv–xcv, printed in *CLBD*, 192–208.
16 Doyle, 'An Unrecognized Piece of Piers the Ploughman's Creed', 431.

French negated finite verbs with preceding *ne*. Therefore, a comparison with these Anglo-Norman *ne* particles is necessary. Accordingly we compared the negative finite clauses in the 14th-century Letter-Book D oaths on folios 1r and Dv with the Jubilee Book portion of O.3.11 in order to ascertain whether the *ne* particles in the Jubilee Book are simply a faithful rendering of Anglo-Norman originals. The relevant site is immediately before the finite verb, and these verbs are given in Table 4 in the Appendix, along with an explanation of the dating of the Letter-Book D oaths. We found that out of the thirteen Anglo-Norman *ne* particles negating finite verbs in the 14th-century oaths on folios 1r and Dv of Letter-Book D, only two are replicated in the corresponding 15th-century Jubilee Book versions. The other eleven are modernised, e.g.

> Mayor's Oath, Letter-Book D, f. 1r: *si vo^9 ne poez faire*
> O.3.11, f. 136v: *if ye may nat do it*

where the *ne* particle is omitted and an English *nat* negator is inserted. These Anglo-Norman oaths were not simply calqued particle-for-particle into English, and there are six instances where the Hammond scribe places a negator *ne* particle in front of finite verbs which do not have precedents in the earlier Letter-Book D oaths. These *ne*s are mainly in the extra clauses in the oaths of the mayor and aldermen.[17] The most parsimonious explanation for this is that his exemplar for these extra clauses was written in 14th-century English, in which negator *ne* was still variably present.

ON FINITE-VERB POSITION IN THE EXTRA CLAUSES

The extra clauses in the oaths of the mayor and aldermen beg the question: was the whole of the Jubilee Book originally conceived of and written up in English, or was it a translation of an earlier text originally composed in Anglo-Norman (which is the language of the earliest oaths, in the 14th-century hand of Letter-Book D folios 1r and Dv), with extra material added in English 1377–83 (which is when the Jubilee Book is dated internally)? In other words, does the text of the extra clauses differ from the rest of the text? To answer this question we compared the language of the extra clauses in the oaths of the mayor, recorder, aldermen and sheriff in O.3.11, given in bold in Table 5 in the appendix, with the rest of the text in those oaths.[18] English is a subject–verb–object language, but Medieval Latin had the property of finite-verb placement

---

[17] These clauses are: Mayor's Oath, f. 136v, 'ye **ne** doo anon levie'; Aldermen's Oath, f. 144r, 'altho whiche **ne** wern nat … sworn', f. 144r, 'if he **ne** have no Resonable encheason', f. 144r, 'if ther **ne** be Clerk', f. 144v, 'if ther **ne** be any difficulte'; Sheriff's Sergeants' Oath, f. 149r, 'yee **ne** do'.

[18] Etymology is of no help here as although the extra clauses retain Anglo-Norman vocabulary, so do all legal texts of 14th- and 15th-century date.

34

at the end of the clause, although this was a variable rule as Latin word order was to some extent free. The mayor's, recorder's, aldermen's and sheriff's oaths (and the rest of folios 133–155 of O.3.11) show both English subject–verb–object order and the latinate object–subject–verb order. For example:

> ne non extorcioun) to any psone poore ne Riche bi colo⁷ of youre office yee shul doo

versus

> And þat yee shalbe tendre of Right of Orphans to save

where *shul* sits at the end of the clause in the first illustration, but *shal* sits at the beginning of the clause in the second.[19] Therefore, we counted ratios of subject–verb–object to object–subject–verb placement in both the extra clauses and the rest of those oaths, on the grounds that had the extra clauses been inserted at a later time, different choices with regard to finite-verb position in the clause could have been made.

Table 2: Finite-verb position in mayor's, aldermen's, recorder's and sheriff's oaths in O.3.11

	subject–verb–object	*object–subject–verb*
extra clauses in mayor's, aldermen's, recorder's and sheriff's oaths in O.3.11	19 (49%)	20 (51%)
rest of mayor's, aldermen's, recorder's and sheriff's oaths in O.3.11	33 (41%)	47 (59%)

These ratios are not sufficiently divergent to suggest that the extra clauses were added later, or by someone else, or in another language, or under any other differing circumstances.

---

19 Free variation in finite-verb placement can be seen by comparing *that this to yow be more soun) sent* (Recorder's Oath, f. 142v, and Aldermen's Oath, f. 143v) with *that this be to yow more Rather sent* (Sheriff's Oath, f. 147v), where 'to you' precedes the finite verb 'be' in the first, but follows the finite verb 'be' in the second. The adverbial 'well and truly' (calquing *bien & loiaument vo͛ au͛ez* in the Anglo-Norman versions) demonstrates all positions: subject–verb–object: *ye shal wele and triewly do* (Mayor's Oath, f. 136v); object–subject–verb: *wele and triewly yee shul f've* (Aldermen's Oath, f. 143); subject–object–verb: *yee wele and triewly kepe* (Sheriff's Oath, f. 147v). It is true that the Jubilee Book versions of the mayor's, recorder's, aldermen's and sheriff's oaths are substantially word-for-word translations of the earlier Letter-Book D folios Dv and 1r versions, but there is sufficient discrepancy for this comparison of word order to be worth undertaking, e.g. *vr͛e peyne mettres/put yow in peyne, droit freez/yee do Right* (Mayor's Oath); *p͛st s͛rez/ye shalbe Redy, tendre s͛rez/yee shalbe tendre* (Aldermen's Oath) – versus *tendre shalbe* (Recorder's Oath, f. 143); *dreiture frez/yee do Right, prestz serrez/yee shalbe Redy* (Sheriff's Oath).

CONCLUSION

Doyle observed that the Hammond scribe's translations (in Worcester F.172, but it is also true of O.3.11) are 'unique renderings, done so literally as to depend on the originals for intelligibility', but it is word-stem and word-order that provoke this characterisation rather than morphology. We interpret the Hammond scribe's wording not as a bad translation of Anglo-Norman but as a legal, administrative one. The originator of the text invented an English-language register of governance whereby the original Anglo-Norman wording can be reverse-engineered. It was a matter of proceeding, as lawyers do, conservatively and with caution: the first step in establishing English as a medium for written legal record was to translate the morphology (the smallest units of grammar, the word-endings, prepositions, negators) but to keep the rest of the text – the wordstock – as faithful as possible to the Anglo-Norman exemplar. Anglo-Norman word-stems still perdure in the legal register to this day. So far as we can see from the analysis above, folios 133–155 of O.3.11 were rendered into English in the period 1377–83. This conclusion is based on:

a) a comparison of the distribution of negative *ne* particles throughout O.3.11, finding a higher number in texts dated to the 14th century, leading to a conclusion that the Hammond scribe's Jubilee Book exemplar was composed in the 14th century.

b) the relationship of *ne* particles in English oaths in folios 133–155 to *ne* particles in earlier, similar, 14th-century Anglo-Norman oaths in Letter-Book D folios 1r and Dv. The relationship was found to be not identical – the English and French *ne*s do not directly correspond. Extra material in the Jubilee Book versions not present in the Letter-Book D versions also contain *ne* particles, suggesting that the Hammond scribe's exemplar was written at a time when *ne* particles were still in use in English.

c) a comparison of ratios of finite-verb position in these oaths' extra material, which were found to be relatively similar to the rest of the oaths. There is no reason to assume that the additions were not contemporaneous with the composition of the rest of the oaths.

Finally, limitations: the variable *ne*s in folios 133–155 of O.3.11 (including the extra clauses) indicate an underlying date of composition in English in the 14th century – which is indeed commensurate with the hypothesis that they constitute the Jubilee Book – but we reserve the position that it is not proof.

APPENDICES

1. Table 3: Distribution of negative-tensed verbs with and without preceding particle ne *in O.3.11*

Conjunction *ne* is not included in the comparison because conjunction *ne* was still current in the 1480s when the Hammond scribe was operative (dating by the church watermark), in contradistinction to negator *ne* which had fallen out of use by then. Conjunction *ne* sometimes doubles as a negator; these have been excluded from the count.

Folios	*Contents*	*−ne*	*+ne*
1v–7	Preface and contents of *De Moneta*	18/18 (100%)	0
7–25	*De Moneta*	81/81 (100%)	0
26–45	Charter of the City of London	35/35 (100%)	0
61–65	Of the Liberties and Franchises in the City of London in the time of Saint Edward	7/7 (100%)	0
67–86	'Auncient Customs that the kyng ought to take of Marchaundices in london'	20/25 (80%)	5 (20%)
87–96	Laws governing the London Sheriff's Court: 'Of the Shereves Court daies'	20/41 (49%)	21 (51%)
100–100v	The Statute of Servants made the 24th year of King Edward III	1/3 (33%)	2 (67%)
100v–103	Plaints, pleas and definitions of legal terms	4/6 (67%)	2 (33%)
103–122	Legal casebook – texts, precedents, cases	8/15 (53%)	7 (47%)
133–155	'The newe booke of thauncient customs and vsages in the Citee of London' (*Jubilee Book*)	63/109 (58%)	46 (42%)
155v–157	Charters	4/4 (100%)	0

2. Table 4: Comparison of ne particles in negative finite clauses in the Letter-Book D oaths and O.3.11 oaths

Sharpe says that the oaths written on the flyleaves to Letter-Book D are 15th-century,[20] and this is true of the oaths written on folios A–D. However, folios D verso and 1 recto are written in 14th-century hands, and are copies of oaths that predate the Jubilee Book.

```
Dv    E                    F     1r
 |     |_____|     |
 |_____|
```

The book has been rebound in modern times: flyleaves A, B and C are of similar size, and E and F is a bifolium sewn with blue thread inserted between D and the first folio of the text, 1 (without taking the book apart it is not possible to determine further the original quiring of the flyleaves). The oaths included in the body of Letter-Book D (folios 85–96, 15th-century hand) were copied onto the blank recto of folio 1 (the book starts on the verso) and, when these oaths needed updating, flyleaves were added in front, so that updated copies could be positioned at the beginning of the book. The flyleaf oaths therefore run backwards in date order, with the most recent, from the 15th century, on flyleaf A, and the earliest, from the 14th century, on the recto of folio 1. Folios D verso and 1 recto contain the earliest oaths. Thus the sequence runs: Letter-Book D, folios 1r and Dv (earlier 14th century); Jubilee Book (1377–83); *Liber Albus* (early 15th century); Letter-Book D other flyleaves and folios 85–96 (later 15th century). If this interpretation is correct, then on internal dating, folio Dv (oath of sheriffs) and folio 1r (oath of the recorder) swear loyalty to Edward III, who reigned 1327–77; and folio Er (oath of sheriffs) and folio Ev (oath of the recorder) swear loyalty to Edward IV, who reigned 1461–70 and 1471–83.

Table 4 shows a comparison of *ne* particles in negative finite clauses in the Letter-Book D oaths and the Jubilee Book. \ / indicates text inserted above the line. Folios in Letter-Book D are numbered 1, D, E, F, recto (r) and verso (v). The folio number is given before the textual extract, so that Er, for example, refers to the recto side of flyleaf E.

[20]   *CLBD*, II, n. 4.

Oath	Letter-Book D	Letter-Book D	Jubilee Book
Mayor	ɪ ʀ Ne **ne** assentͤez au destrees	Ev Ne **ne** assentͤez au destrees	136v and ['*ye* Ø *shall' omitted*] nat assente to distres
	ɪ ʀ si voͦ **ne** poez faire	Ev et si vous **ne** poez faire	136v if ye Ø may nat do it
	ɪ ʀ tort **ne** freez a nuly	Ev tort **ne** frez a nulli	136v no wrong that yee Ø do
	ɪ ʀ riens **ne** pͦndrez pˣ qī le Roi pde	Ev rienz **ne** pͦndrez p q̑i le Roi pde	136v nothyng Ø take bi the whiche þᵗ kyng leese
			136v ye **ne** doo anon levie
Recorder	ɪ ʀ **ne** descouereez	Ev **ne** descouͤeez	142v yee Ø shal nat discovere
	ɪ ʀ voͦ **ne**/ lerreez pˣ doun	Ev vous **ne** lerreez pˣ doun	142v yee Ø shul nat lette for yitfᵗ
	ɪ ʀ nul iugement **ne** targerez	Ev nul jugement **ne** targerez	142v no iugement ye **ne** torne
		E+r rien **ne** prendrez	142v no yift … yee Ø shal take
		E+r nuⱧ fees ne robes **ne** pͦndrez de nully	142v no fees ne Robes … ye Ø shul nat bere were ne take
			yee Ø shul nat assente
			yee Ø shal nat gyve
			yee Ø shul nat do

Oath	Letter-Book D	Letter-Book D	Jubilee Book
Aldermen	ɪr si voꝰ **ne** soiez … desturbe	F vous **ne** soiez … desturbez	143v if yee **ne** be … distroubled
		F voꝰ **ne** vendrez nuⱖ manꝰe vitaille	
			143v yee Ø shal nat assente
			143v clothyng Ø be nat yeven
			144r no seisyn … Ø be … delivered
			144r altho whiche **ne** wern nat … sworn
			144r if he **ne** have no Resonable encheason
			144r if he **ne** be Clerk
			144v if ther **ne** be any difficulte
Sheriffs			147r **ne** yee Ø shuln lete non to maynpise
	Dv nule bone custume **ne** abaterez	Er nule bone custume **ne** abaterez	147v no gode custom yee Ø abate
	Dv nule male **ne** leuerez	Er nuⱖ male Ø leuꝰez	147v non evil yee Ø levie
	Dv les Jugiementz … **ne** targerez	Er les jugementz … **ne** targerez	147v the iugementes … ye Ø tarie nat
	Dv les briefs … **ne** retꝛnerez	Er les Briefs … **ne** retꝛnerez	147v the writtis … yee Ø Retourne nat
			147v no yift … ye Ø take
			147v ye Ø shul nat assent
	Dv **ne** … lerres a ferme	Er **ne** … lerrez a ferme	147v yee Ø shuln nat leete to ferme

40

Oath	Letter-Book D	Letter-Book D	Jubilee Book
Sheriff's Clerks		Fv vous **ne** lerrez p² doun	148r yee Ø lette nat for yift
		Fv vous **ne** seoffretz	148r yee **ne** suffre
		Fv nul iugement **ne** targerez	148v no iugement Ø be taried
		Fv vous **ne** seoffres voz fermers p̊ndre	148v yee Ø suffre nat your fermers to take
		Fv les brefs … **ne** retou◇anant	148v the writtis … yee Ø shuln nat Return
		Fv qils **ne** p̊ignent plus de cariage	148v thei Ø take nomore to cariage
		Fv **ne** qils greuent les gentz	148v thei **ne** greve nat the people
			148v yee Ø shal nat yielde
			148v if it Ø be nat
Sheriff's Sergeants			149r yee **ne** do
			149r yee Ø shuln nat tarie
		Er vous **ne** vendrez nul mane vitaille	
Total *ne*	13/13 (100%)	23/24 (96%)	10/43 (23%)

Bold type indicates that there is no equivalent passage in the other text.

Oath	Letter-Book D (14th century)	O.3.11 (15th century)
Mayor	f. 1r: Vð iurrez qe bien & loiaument ſuirez \nrᵉe seignᵛ/ le Roi en office du Meiraute en la Citee de Loundres . Et mesme la Cite garderez seurement & sauuement al oeps le Roi Dengleᵗre & de ses heyrs Rois Dengleᵗre & le prou le Roi freez en tothes choses q̃ a vð apendent afaire . Et les droitures le Roi en gᵘuge a la Coroune appendent en la dite Citee . loiaument garderez . Ne ne assenſez au destrees ne au concelement des droitz ne des fraunchises le Roi . Et p̃ la ou vð sauᵉz les droitz le Roi **ou de la Coroune soit en ᵉtres ou en rentes ou en fraunchises ou en suytes concelees ou soustretes** . vrᵉe peyne mettres de ceo repeller . et si vð ne poez faire . ' vð le dirrez au Roi ou a ceux de son conseil desq̃x vð soiez ꝯteyn q̃ eux le dirront au Roi . ' Et q̃ loialment & a droiture treterez le poeple de vrᵉe baillie & droit freez a chescun . ' auxi bien a estranges . ' com a p̃uez a poures com a Riches en ceo q̃ a vð appent afaire . Et q̃ p̃ᵃ hauteste ne p̃ᵃ Richeste ne p̃ᵃ doun ne p̃ᵃ p̃messe ne p̃ᵃ fauour ne p̃ᵃ hayour tort ne freez a nuly ne nuly droiture destourberez ne riens ne p̃ndrez p̃ᵃ q̃ĩ le Roi p̃de . ' ou p̃ᵃ q̃ĩ droiture soit destourbee Et q̃ en totes choses q̃ au meire de la dite Citee appendent afayre . ' si dieu vð eyed & les seintz.	f. 136v: yE shal swere that weele and triewly yee shal ſᵛe our lord the kyng in the office of mairolte in the Citee of london and the same Citee kepe sauf and sure to thuse of the kyng of Ingland and of his heires of Inglond and the profite of the kyng fressh in al thynges that to yow appendith ye shuln do And the kynges Rightis in eᵛiche that to the Corowne appendip in the saide Citee triewly ye shal kepe and nat assente to distres ne to concele or huyde the kynges Rightis and fraunchises // And bi ther wher ye knowe the kynges right be withdrawe . ye shul put yow in peyne this to Repelle . and if ye may nat do it ye shul do telle it vnto the kyng or to theym that bien of his counsail of whom ye bien in ᵂay certeynte that thei wil telle it vnto the kyng // And that triewly and Rightwisly ye treate the people in your baile **without extorcioun⟩ to any doyng bi colour of yoᵃ office** // And that yee do Right to eᵛiche aswel to straungiers as to Densyns to pore as to Riche in asmoche as appendith in yow to do and p̃ᵃ for no highnesse ne for Richesse . for yift ne for pmyse for fauour ne for hate . no wrong that yee do to any . ne no Right disturbe ne nothyng take bi the whiche p̃ᵃ kyng leese his Right or any Right bi that be distᵒbled **And that ye be tendre and take heede to the Rightſ of Orphans and of the Chambre to save and to mayntene after the lawes and vsages of the Citee ne suffre non Orphan to be maried withyn age . that ye ne doo anon levie the peyne vpon that ordeigned the þ And þᵃ y ben tendre to al the ordynaunces withyn this booke in al their articles and theym susteyne to youre power ne assent without the comune counsail of the saide Citee to any ordynaunces or jugementis contrarie to that** // And in in al thynges that to the Maire of the Citee appendith ye shal wele and triewly do and by have yow so God yow help and al seyntis

Oath	Letter-Book D (14th century)	O.3.11 (15th century)
Recorder	f. 1r: voˢ iurreetz qe voˢ serreez foials & loials au Roy Edward Dengleᵗe & as ses heirs & a la Citee de loundres . et les ffraunchises & vsages de mesme la Citee deynz ville & de hors solonc vrᵉe poair meyntendreez . & le conseyl de mesme la Citee ne descouerez . et qe voˢ \ne/ lerreez pᵗ doun ne pᵗ fauour ne pᵗ ᵱmes ne pᵗ haiour qe owele ley & droiture freez as totes maneres des gentz si bien as poures come as riches pᵗuez come estraunges qe deuaunt voˢ plederenzes en pleez hustengals & en totes autres maneres des plees . et totes les pleez qe deuaunt voˢ serront pledeez loialment les recorderez & vrᵉe diligence mettereez de sᵘuer qe les ditz pleez soient bien & loialment enroules ne nuly droiture destourbereez . et qe nul iugement ne targerez saunz resonable enchesoun . Et si voˢ sauerez les droitz ou ᵱfitz \du Roy ou/ de la dite Citee come en ᵗres rentes tenementz ou forprises southtretes ou concelez .ᵗ voˢ les moustrez as meire & Auderm̃ pᵗ les droitᵗes de mesme \le Roy &/ la Citee sauuer .ᵗ et ᵖstement vendrez as garnissementz du meire & viscounts ou de lour ministres pᵗ bon & seiñ) consail a eux doner pᵗ lestat de la dite Citee garder & meintener . et en toutes autres choses qe a vrᵉe office appendent affaire .ᵗ bien & loialment voˢ en auerez si dieu voˢ eide & les saintz	ff. 142v–143: E shal swere that yee shalbe feithful and true to the kyng of Inglond and to his heires . and to the Citee of london and the fraunchices and vsages of the same Citee withyn the Citee and withoute after yowe power yee shal mayntene and the counsail of the saide Citee yee shal nat discovere and that yee shul nat lette for yitfᵗ ne for fauoᵗ ne for ᵱmyse ne for hate that evene lawe and Right yee shal do to al maner of people aswel to pore as to Riche Denisyn as straungier that bifore yow shal pleate in plees hustynges and in alother maner of plees // And that al bᵉ plees that bifore yow shalbe pleated triewly ye shal Recorde and youᵗ diligence sette and oversee . that the saide plees bien wele and triewly enrolled ne no Right distroubled And that no iugement ye ne tarie withoute Resonable encheason // And if yee knowe the Rightes or the profites of the Citee as in londis tenementis Rentis forprised wᵗ drawen conceled or hid . yee shul shewe to the Maire and Aldermen for the Rightes of the same Citee to save // And Redily to come at the warnyng of the Maire or Shereves or of their Ministres . for goode and holsum counsail hem to yeve for the state of the Citee to kepe and maynten // **And tendre shalbe to the Rightes of Orphans to save and to mayntene after the lawes and vsages of the Citee // ne no yift of any psone grete ne smal yee shal take if yee trowe bi youre conscience that this be to yow more souᵗ sent for mayntenaunce of sum quarel or for to distroudle or delaie the Right of any than for any other love or friendship // Ne no fees ne Robes of any foreyn lord ne of nonoᵖ ye shul nat bere were ne take duryng yoᵗ office // And al thordynaunces in this booke in al their articles triewly yee shul susteyne ne to any ordynaunces contrarie to thiese yee shul nat assente ne iugement to the contᵃry yee shal nat gyve without assent of the comune counsail of the Citee ne non extorciouⁿ) to any psone poore nor Riche bi colour of yoᵗ office yee shul nat do // And in alother thynges that to your office appenden to do yee wele and triewly shalbe have yow so god help yow and al seyntis**

Oath	Letter-Book D (14th century)	O.3.11 (15th century)
Aldermen	f. 11: Vo⁹ iurez q̃ bien & loiaument s̃uerez \nr̃ᵉ seign⁷/ le Roi en la Citee \de Londr⁹s/ en le office de Alderman en la garde de . N . ou vo⁹ estes Alderman eslu & loiaument tret̃ez & enfourm̃ez les gentz de mesme la garde deschoses q̃ a eux apenderes a faire p̃ la garde de la Citee & p̃ la pees en la Citee meynten̄ . et q̃ les leys vsages & fraunchises de la dite Citee garderez meyntenderez **& defendrez** deinz ville & de hors solonc vr̃ᵉ sen & poair & q̃ tendre s̃rez des droites des orphanyns sau̯ & meyntener surlan les leys & usages de la dite Citee/ et q̃ p̃st s̃rez & p̃stement vendrez a les somounses & garnissementz du meire & ministres de la Citee q̃ p̃ temps s̃ront . ' p̃ les assises pleetz & iugementz hustengals & autres bosoynges de la Citee espleit̃ ' . si vo⁹ ne soiez p̃ les bosoynges nr̃ᵉ seign⁷ le Roi ou p autre resnable encheson desturbe & q̃ bon & leal conseil durrez a les choses tochantz cõmun p̃fit en mesme la Citee et q̃ bien & loiaument vo⁹ au̯ez en le dit office & autres choses tochantz la Citee . ' si dieu vo⁹ eyed & les seintz.	ff. 143–143v: E shal swere that wele and triewly yee shul f̃ve the kyng and the Citee of london in the office of Alderman in the warde of whiche yee be Alderman chosen and triewly yee shuln entreate and enfo⁹rme the people of the same warde of þinges that appenden hem to do for the garde **and kepyng** of the Citee and for the pees in the Citee to mayntene And that the lawes and vsages and fraunchices of þᵉ saide Citee yee kepe and mayntene withyn the Citee and withoute after yo⁹ connyng and power And þat yee shalbe tendre of Right of Orphans to save and to mayntene after the lawes and vsages of the saide Citee // And that ye shalbe Redy . and Redily come at þᵉ somons and warnyng of the Maire and Ministres of the saide Citee that for the tyme shuln be for thasises plees and iugementƺ hustynges and other nedis of the Citee to be emploied if yee ne be for the needis of our lord þᵉ kyng or bi other Resonable encheason distroubled And þat goode . lawful and triew counsail yee yeve to the thynges touchyng the comune profite in the Same Citee **ne no yift of any psone grete ne smal ye take if yee trowe bi yo⁹ conscience that this to yow be more sounᴰ sent for mayntenaunce of any quarel or for to distourbe or delay the Right of any than for other love or friendship And al thordynaunces in this booke in al their articles triewly yee shul sustene ne to any ordynaunces or iugement contrarie to thiese yee shal nat assente without the comune counsail of the Citee // And that due execuciounᴰ of presentementƺ in yo⁹ wardmote yee shuln doo and ententiefly pursue ne non extorciounᴰ to any psone poore ne Riche bi colo⁹ of youre office yee shul doo** And that wele and triewly yee shul be have yow in the saide office and al other thynges wherof yee shul ent̃mete touchyng the saide Citee so god yow help and al seyntes

Oath	Letter-Book D (14th century)	O.3.11 (15th century)
Sheriff	f. Dv: Uous iurez qe uous serrez fels e loiaux au Roi Edward \Dengleťře/ e a ses heirs e la fraunchise de Loundres sauuerez e meintendrez deinz ville e de hors solom vŕe poer. E qe bien & loialment garderez les Countez de Loundŕ's e de Middelsex. Et les offices qe a mesme les Countez aptent afere .' bien & loialment frez solom vŕe sen . e vŕe poer. Et qe dreiture frez ausibien a poures come a riches . E qe nule bone custume ne abaterez ne nule male ne leuerez . E qe les assises de pain & de čuoise & des totes autres assises qe a vous appendent deinz la ffraunchise de la Cite & de hors .' bien & loialment garderez et frez garder. E qe les Jugiementz & les Execucions de vŕe Court ne targerez saunz resnable encheson .' ne nuli dreiture destorberez E qe les briefs qe a uous venent tochantz lestat & la fraunchise de la Cite ne ret'nerez .' auant ceo qe les eiez moustre au Meire qi p' temps serra & al conseil de la Cite & qe de eux eiez auisement . E qe prestz serrez a les resnables garnisementz du Meire .' p' la pees e lestat de la Cite garder & meintenir . E qe totes les autres choses qe appendent al office & a la garde des ditz Countez loialment frez par vous & les voz .' & la dite Cite garderez de damage solom vŕe sen & vŕe poer. E qe le Counte de Middelsex ne la garde de la gaole de Neugate lerres a ferme si dieu v⁹ eide & les seintz .	ff. 147–148: yE shuln swere that yee shuln be feithful and triewe to our lord the kyng and to his heires kynges and the fraunchise of the Citee of londoñ) yee shul save and mayntene withyn the Citee and wt out after your power . and that yee be obeisaunt vnto the Maire that for the tyme shalbe and tho that shuln be arrested bi the Maire and Aldermen yee shuln sende to oon of yoˀ Compto's saufly to be kept ne yee shuln lete non to maynp'se without thassent of the Maire or of that Alderman and at Resonable comaundement of the Maire ye shulln be obedient and that yee wele and triewly kepe the Countees and Shuyres of london and Middilsexˀ // And thoffices . that to the same Shires apperteynen to do wele and triewly . yee shuln doo after yowre connyng and power . And that yee do Right aswel to poore as to Riche without any extorsiouñ) doyng to any psone bi coloˀ of yoˀ office And that no gode custom yee abate . ne non evil yee levie or a Reise And that thassises of brede and Ale and alother assises that to yow apperteynen withyn the fraunchice of the Citee and without wele and triewly yee shuln kepe and do to be kept // And that the iugementes and execucions of your court ye tarie nat without resonable encheasoun . ne no Right yee distrouble // And that the writis that shuln come to yow touchyng thestate and the fraunchice of the Citee . yee Retourne nat afore that yee have shewed hem to the Maire and Aldermen that for the tyme shuln bien and to the counsail of the saide Citee if neede be . and that of hem yee have avisement . and that yee shalbe Redy at Resonable warnyng of the Maire for the pees and thestate of the Citee to be kept and mayntened // And that no yift of any psone lasse ne more ye take if ye trowe bi your conscience that this be to yow more Rather sent for mayntenaunce of any quarel or for to distourbe or delay the Right of any man pan for any other love or frienchip // And al thordynaunces in this booke in al their articles triewly yee shuln susteyne ne to any ordynaunces or iugementis contrarie to this without the comune counseil of the Citee ye shul nat assent And that the Shyre of Middilsexˀ ne the kepyng of the jail of Newgate yee shuln nat leete to ferme . and that alother thynges that apperteynen to your office and the kepyng of the saide Shyres truly yee shuln do bi yow and bi yowres // And the saide Citee ye shuln kepe from damage after yoˀ konnyng and power // And the half of fynes of fraies of bloode shed Risyng in your tyme to the Chambrelayn truly . yee shuln delivere or do to be delyvered // And that . yee han nomo than .iiij. ffauntis and that wele and . triewly yee shuln be have yow in the saide office and alother thynges wherof yee entremeten touchyng the saide Citee so god yow help and al seyntis

EDITORIAL METHOD

In the following transcription we have attempted to retain as much of the Hammond scribe's original layout as possible, including abbreviation and suspension symbols and paragraph markers. However, line-length and word-division has not been retained other than on the torn page, in order to convey the shape of the tear. <...> indicates matter that is illegible. Italicised text in the margin indicates the flyleaf hand. Numbers in the margin are aligned with relevant clauses as in the manuscript. Abbreviation and suspension symbols are reproduced so far as is possible in modern type, and capitalisation attempts to represent the original. Verso foliation numbers have been added as the manuscript is foliated in a modern hand in Arabic numerals on recto only, and the original Roman folio numbers have been retained. Trinity College, Cambridge, MS O.3.11 has been digitised and is viewable at the Wren Digital Library website, https://mss-cat.trin.cam.ac.uk/Manuscript/O.3.11.

In the Translation, the outward appearance of the MS has been abandoned, although the paragraph numbering of the original has been retained. Editorial additions and explanations are indicated by square brackets [ ].

Rich: 2

133

Cxxxiij.

La proheme de ł The probleme in the newe booke of thauncient customs and vsages in the Citee of london compiled and affermed bi the Maire Aldermen and Comunes of the same Citee the yeer⁹ of kyng Richard the secunde the first yeer⁹

he pfeccioun̄) of al policie and the grounde of   *//. j.*

t   goode gou̇naunce dwellen and abiden vpon .ij.

thynges the whiche ne mown nat be disseu̇ed

ne departed but alwey to guyder to be hold and kept ffirst

that the sages and Rightwis gou̇nours of the Comune people in

their gou̇naunce in their Reddure and fauoˀ after this that the

tyme Requireth so be it demaunded and modified // Secunda   *//. ij.*

rily that the comune people be tretable and of oon accord and

bi deꝼvyng loven they their gou̇nours and sou̇aignes and

that thei of hem han dreede and theym obeyen the whiche

.ij. thynges aforsaide wele and stidefastly kept on that oo

part and that other every Citee shalbe sette in h

and tranquillite // And for this that the C

is the pʳncipal Citee of the Realme of

in gou̇nail to al the Realme after

de Rule and gou̇naunce than

Realme for to yeve ensampl

nours and the comunalte

holden eche in estate a

after this that is

and nurisshed a

Fabian   Nicholas B

chr p.   Twiford a

Cxli   Adam of

        Walwor

        and ma

        Craft

        of G

        gers

        Pe

133v Irmongers . Smythes . loryms⁹ . haberdasshers . lethersellers
Masons . Carpentiers . Bochiers . Cordewans⁹ . Curriours
Tanns⁹ . whitawiers . Bowiers . ffletchiers . Sporiers . horns⁹
webbis . ffullers . Diers . Shermen . Glovers powchemakers
ffoundours . Brasiers . wexchaundeliers . Talghchaundeliers
hurers. hatters. ffuystours . joynours . woodemongers . To꞉no꞉s
Cowpers . julers . and . Pater nosters or makers of beedis
the whche psones aforsaide consideryng many goode article₃
touchyng the p͏ᵣncipal gou͏ꞌnaunce of the saide Citee and
the goode customs and auncient vsages of the same to be in
dyus⁹ grete bookes of the same Citee comprised and that
grete labour and diligence was to serche and seeke in tymes
covenable . and of whiche the comunes of the saide Citee
ne mown nat be at a ɏay certeinte without Right grete
costages to officers ordeigned . and of oon accorde thei han .
<a>ssentid that al the articles ensuyng to the hono꞉ of god
ne profite Rest and tranquillite of the saide Citee
Realme shalbe compiled in the forme that
th // And upon this aswele the above
Aldermen and Comuners as the
in name and bi consent of al
vpon the holy Euᵃngelice to
e articles ensuyng for
we outrageouse
en often in grete
e day that þᵉ
that the sur
he saide Citee
wher þem
d whom
Maire
Guyld
lect
so al

wey that the grettest craftes ne cheesen nomo than .vj. psones
the measne Craftes .iiij. and the lest .ij. psones the whiche .
shuln dwel dure and abide for the yeer⁹ folowyng in that of
counsail without eschaunge if deth or other wey and reasonable
cause nat excuse And if any thyng be ordeigned bi the Maire
and aldermen that toucheth the comunalte . without thassent
of theym chosen or of the gretter partie of hem or at the lest
.xij. of the most sufficient craftes þᵗ that ordynᵃnce be hold for
nought //
And that altho so chosen be charged bi oth in the man͏ᵉe that
ensueth that is to wite

134
Cxxxiiij
V. Fab.
Chrō in
R. John
anno iii.
choice of
the Coṁ
councel by
// .iiij. yᵉ
Crafts of
yᵉ City

48

Thoth of theym that bien chosen for þe côen counsaile

y E shuln swere that yee bien Redy to come whan yee shuln be somoned for the comune counsail and goode counsail ye shuln yeve after yowr wisdam and knowlache and for no fauoꝛ to mayntene any singular profit agenst þe profite of the Citee savyng to eu̸y craft their resonable vsagis and whan yee be so comen yee shul nat departe without resonable cause or licence of the Maire or bifore that the Maire and his felawship departe so god yow help and al seyntis // //. j.

And if any craft faile of Retornyng the names of his craft to the Maire the day that he shalbe charged of his Mairalte the people of the same Craft to Renne in a m̉ciament of . vj[s] . viij[d] . without any Redempcioun // // .ij.

And that everiche so chosen if he faile to come to þe Guyldhalle at any tyme whan thei shuln be warned or somoned shal paie .ij[s]. and vpon this be eu̸iche so failyng distressed bi a ſiaunt of the Chambre if his felawship or felawe ne know nat or konne nat of goode feith resonably to be excused and also bien chosen to Retoꝛne to the newe Maire that for the tyme shalbe from yeere vnto yeer⁹ // .iij.

The daies of the Comune counsaile

a lso that eu̸ry quarter of the yeer⁹ or oones in the yeer⁹ at the leste be the Aldermen and the comuners so chosen assembled for to treate and to counsaile vpon the nedis and busynesses of the Citee // .j.

134v and that at that day that the saide somons shalbe assembled ne be ther any pleint attained bitwene partie and partie in the Maires Court nor in the Shereves vpon peyne of the Shereve that doeth to the contrarie of .x. lī to thuse of the Chambre without any Redempcioun //

// .ij. Of whiche the first day shalbe the next ferial that be no day of hustyng after the presentacioun of the newe Maire at the kynges Eschequer or ellis at the Tour //

//. iij. The day of the next quart⁹ shalbe the day of seynt Gregorie the Pope the whiche day ne shal nat be vpon the Soneday for Soneday and for hustyng a cause to lette the Aldermen of their sittyng //

//. iiij. The day of the next quarter ensuyng shalbe the .iiij. Wednysday after Estern // The day of the last quarter shalbe the .iij. day next after the fest of the translacioun of seynt Thomas of Caunterbury if it be nat Soneday or hustyng in this cas the day shalbe holde the next ferial after that Soneday or hustyng //

// .v.   And the day of seynt Mathew whan the Shereves shuln be
chosen agenst whiche day the Maire that for the tyme alwey
thei shuln do to be somoned and ensembled with other of
the . most sufficient of value to the discrecioun) of the Maire
and of the Aldermen the whiche psones so somoned to the
discrecioun) of the maire and Aldermen other than the saide
chosen of craftes whan thei bien cald bi their names bien
entred in the Chambre of comune counsail with the other
chosen thei shuln be sworn bifore the Comunes for than to be
triewe without fraude or malengyne to say their best advise
havyng Regard to no syngulier profite of their friendis but al
vttirly for the comune profite . if he ne be psone that hath born
office in the saide Citee of Alderman or of Shereve the whiche
psone in suche cas shal sey and be charged bi thooth that he
haþ made to the Towne to say and counsaile in the best man⁹
that he can . so as and bi the same man⁹ as other Comuners
that han nat born any suche office bien expssely sworn for
the same silf cause . and also be it don at al tymes that any
Comuners shuln bien assembled with the other chosen for the
comune wele and neede of the Towne and al wey entendyng
what tyme and houre that any grete charge com

withyn the Citee or to the assembles of the chosen any   135
contrausite be bitwene the Maire Aldermen and the chosen of   Cxxxv.
matier that is had amonges hem of theym silf ne mown nat ne
konne nat accorde Than the Maire with thadvise of the more
gretter partie of Aldermen shal do to be somoned of other
comuners of the most sage and most sufficient of the towne to
suche a nombre as the Maire and the saide Aldermen semen
needeful for the matier to come Makyng the saide somoned
whan thei bien with the chosen as is a forsaide //
And at the lest the Maire shal do somone tho chosen at al   //. vj.
tymes that hym semeth expedient and nedeful to take counsail
vpon suche matiers touchyng the comune profite or necessite
of the Citee //
And if it happen that thei com nat all for suche somons .   //. vij.
neutheles if he ther have sum psones of evy craft of the .xij.
most sufficiaunt craftes than the Maire with .viij. Aldermen
and tho that bien psent for the comunalte oughten to procede
in þe matiere needeful and expedient and theym to fynyssh and
bryng to anend but if thei bien so chargeable that they mown
nat be fully entreated wᵗ oute gretter court //

And that al tho so chosen bien thei charged bi þͦ othes the   // viij.
same day that their names bien Retoˀned if thei bien present   *Great*
and if thei bien nat present that thei bien amͦcied if they han   *Court*
nat excusaciou⌒ in marˀ abovesaide and never the lesse bien
they distreyned to come at a certeyn day to take their charge
vpon double peyne . And if any departe withoute licence renne
he in the peyne that he ought to have ronne in if he ha<d> be
somoned and come nat

             lso that non of suche chosen for the tyme that they oc   //. j.
    a   cupien that office shuln nat be put in non enquestes if
             it be nat in plee of lond but ther as where other as suf
ficient ne may nat be founden ne bien they nat made Taxours
ne Collectours of tallages and bien they nat somond nor
coarted to be in comune wacches . but with the Maire Shereves
or Aldermen of þͦ wardes whan thei maken wacches in their
owne propir psone //
And if any Shereve Retoˀne the names of any suche that   //.ij.
occupien . suche office otherwise than is declared above . than
renne he in þᵉ same amͦciament bi distresse of the Maire that
the partie ranne in that so was bi hym Retorned

135v   *The maner of thelleccion of the mayr of london of sent*
        Edwarde̥ day

// j.   lso that eⱴy yeerˀ al the Aldermen bien thei holy as
      a   sembleᵈ at the Guyldhalle in the feste of translaciou⌒
             of seynt Edward and the chosen for the Comunes .
also and other somoned bi thavise of the Maire and Aldermen
for that day . for to cheese a Maire for the yeere than next
ensuyng in the maner that ensueth // The chosen for the
Comons and thoother somoned for that cause shuln be cald bi
a ſiaunt bi their names at a wyndowe that is vpon height of
degrees goyng vp from the Guyldhalle in to the chambre of
the saide Counsail and nonother of the comunes be medlyng in
that chambre wᵗ in that same day but tho so cald bi name vpon
peyne of empʳsoment and so be it don at al tymes . that thei
shuln be assembled for the counsail of the Citee //

// ij.   And the Maire Recordoˀ and Aldermen shuln dwelle and abide
in oon of the baas or low chambres . til than the Comunes
bien avised bi goode deliberaciou⌒ of .ij. psones of whiche
eⱴiche of hem semyth bi their othes to this sufficient and
covenable for to occupie the office of Mairalte for the yeere
next ensuyng //

// iij. And if con^{ta}u^osie a Rise among hem that oon wolde assent
in oo psone and that other . in that other psone be than anon
.ij. côers of the most sufficient chosen bi assent of all whiche
with the comune fiaunt shuln demaunde and aske p^rvily of
e√y psone bi hym silf to the whiche of the .ij. that penden so
in debate they yeven more gladly their assent And ther wher
the gretter partie of nombre is of psones so be that holden for
theleccioun) //

// iiij. And the .ij. côers and the comune fiaunt bien thei charged
bi their faithes that thei nat enforme nor enforce any psone
vpon that deede to do But suffre eche of hem to say freely this
that thei holden at hert for the matier And that triewly they
Reporten whiche of the .ij. hath the more voise //

// v. And whan thei shuln bien in the name of god accorded vpon
.ij. psones thei shuln discende first to the Maire and Aldermen
shewyng to hem their elecciouns and anon thei shuln descende
over in to the Guyldhalle to other comunes if any ther bien
and ther abidyng the Maire and Aldermen bifore the siege of
hustyng til that they comen and therdo þem

to wite vpon whiche of theym .ij. chosen they bien
condescended //
And if he so chosen be he at tha ttyme present or absent be
he redy at the Guyldhalle at the lest at .x. of the Clock in the
feste of Symond and Jude next ensuyng for to take his charge
And if he come nat at the same day be he sent aft⁹ hym that
was named with hym and charged of the office and be it anon
without any tarieng bi the Shereves levied of the goodis londis
Rentis and tenementis withyn the fraunchice of hym that so
absentith CC . li . of sterlynges to thuse of another that bi his
defaute shal so be charged of office without any Remyssioun)
of that to be don) //
And if the secunde so chosen in suche man⁹e be absent in the
feste of seynt Symon and Jude shal paie . CC . li . to thuse of
the chambre and þ^e first of the . CC . li . he shal have that than
// shalbe chosen in their defaute // Purveied alwey and accorded
is that .v. yeere after that a Maire hath accomplisshed a yeer⁹
he ne shal nat be ageyn chosen ne constreyned to be Maire but
if he wil of his owne goode wil
lso as at al tymes that covenable assemble shalbe the
a   comunes that thei bien assembled and cried in
man⁹ abovesaide // And al if any contrauersies
bien bitwene hem moeved and debated touchyng the matiers
for whiche thei bien at that tyme somoned . bien they vsed in
the same man⁹ as it is aforsaide // The penaunce of þem that
comen nat to the comune Counsail

136
Cxxxvj
// vj.

// vij.

// j.

// ij.

52

a   lso that every Alderman be present in the Guyld   // j.
halle in both thaforsaide festis vpon peyne
of .C.ˢ and the chosen for the comunes that that
shuln be somoned for that day vpon peyne of ij.ˢ to paie to
the chambre if they ne han a ƿay excusacioun᷑ bi reason᷑
acceptable //

And the comune ſiaunt shal make a writyng vnto the   // ij.
Chambrelayn of theym that failen bitwene hem endented and
the Chambrelayn shal make levy of al the saide am̊ciamentis
and shal aunswer of theym vpon his accompt and the comune
ſiaunt shal make suche exstrete at al the .vj. daies whiche bien
bifore lymyted in certeyne for to holde the comune counsails
of the

136v   Citee // And the Maire shalbe charged vpon the booke to kepe
// iij.   and to holde thordynaunces in man⁹ that ensuyth

The oth of the Maire

// j.   E shal swere that weele and triewly yee
y   shal ſ́ve our lord the kyng in theoffice of mairolte
in the Citee of london᷑ and the same Citee kepe sauf
and sure to thuse of the kyng of Ingland and of his heires of
Inglond and the profite of the kyng fressh in al thynges that to
yow appendith ye shuln do And the kynges Rightis in eƿiche
that to the Corowne appendiþ in the saide Citee triewly ye
shal kepe and nat assente to distres ne to concele or huyde the
kynges Rightis and fraunchises //

// ij.   And bi ther wher ye knowe the kynges right be withdrawe . ye
shul put yow in peyne this to Repelle . and if ye may nat do
it ye shul do telle it vnto the kyng or to theym that bien of his
counsail of whom ye bien in ƿay certeynte that thei wil telle it
vnto the kyng //

// iij.   And that triewly and Rightwisly ye treate the people in your
baile without extorcioun᷑ to any doyng bi colour of yoˣ
office //

// iiij.   And that yee do Right to eƿiche aswel to straungiers as to
Densyns to pore as to Riche in asmoche as appendith in yow
to do and þᵗ for no highnesse ne for Richesse . for yift ne for
ᵽmyse for fauour ne for hate . no wrong that yee do to any .
ne no Right disturbe ne nothyng take bi the whiche þᵗ kyng
leese his Right or any Right bi that be distˢbled //

// v.   And that ye be tendre and take heede to the Rightͤ of Orphans
and of the Chambre to save and to mayntene after the lawes
and vsages of the Citee ne suffre non Orphan to be maried
withyn age . that ye ne doo anon levie the peyne vpon that
ordeigned ~~the þ~~ And þᵗ y ben tendre to al the ordynaunces
withyn this booke in al their articles and theym susteyne to
youre power ne assent without the comune counsail of the
saide Citee to any ordynaunces or jugementis contrarie to

53

that //

And in in al thynges that to the Maire of the Citee appenden   // vj.
ye shal wele and triewly do and by have yow so god yow help
and al seyntis   whan the gen⁹al Court of the Maire shalbe
holden

          lso that the Maire hold his general Court so   // j.
a   alwey as hath bien vsed the moneday next
        after the feste of the Epiphany At which Court shalbe
al the Aldermen and Shereves pʳsent and the Ministres of eʋy
warde if they ne have no ʋay excusacioun̄ That is to wite
Conestables Scavageours and Bedils whiche shuln be charged
ther in presence of the Maire nat withstandyng any charge
that thei han made or don bifore their Aldermen And if any
Alderman be absent at that Court without due excusacioun̄
shal paie .C.ˢ to thissue of the Maire / and the Ministre absent
shal paie .ij.ˢ wherof the comune ſiaunt shal make an estrite to
the Chambrelayn in fourme abovesaide //

And if any Alderman or other Ministre present in that Court   // ij.
any trespas don in their wardis agenst the pees of the kyng
or agenst any ordynaunce of the Citee . that anon þᵉ culpable
be distressed to come to aunswer or arrested bi his body if he
have nat wherof to be distressed and taken to suche issue as
the lawe and vsages of the Citee Requiren / And that non of
the Shereves deliveren ne leten to maynprise suche culpables
withoute the assent of the Maire and Aldermen vpon peyne of
.C.ˢ to the chamber //

And if any Alderman afforce hym silf to mayntene suche a   // iij.
malfesour and mysdoer . at the first tyme shal paie .xx.ˢ and at
the secunde tyme .xl.ˢ And if he ne cease for the amⁱciamentis
be he put out from thoffice of Alderman //

And if any Minist⁹ or other do any thyng lik shal paie at the   // iiij.
first tyme dj̄ a mᵃrc and at another tyme .j. mᵃrc and at the
thrid tyme leese his fraunchise and office //

And the Maire shal do   // v.

137ᵛ

due execucioun̄ in that and in al plaintes that shuln be put
bifore hym in that Court without respite doyng to any

The oth of Conestables

// j.

         E shuln swer that ye shul kepe the pees of oure
y   lord the kyng wele and triewly after yowre
        power and ye shuln arrest altho that maken conteck
Riot . debate or affray in brekyng of þᵉ kynges pees and hym
to leede to the house or comptoˀ of sum of the Shereves
and if ye be withstonde bi force of any suche . mysdoers ye
shuln levie vpon hem hugh and cry and . theym to pursue
from streate to streate and from warde til warde til thei bien
arrested //

54

// ij.   And also ye shuln serche at altymes whan yee shuln be
Required of Scavageours or of Bedils the comons nat beyng of
þᵉ warde and the defautes that yee fynde yee shuln presente to
the Maire and to the Ministres of the Citee //

// iij.   And if yee be distroubled bi any psones that ye mow nat
doo yoᵗ office duely ye shuln certifie to the Maire and to þᵉ
counsail of the Citee the name or the names of hym or theym
that yow han distroubled //

// iiij. And this ye shul nat lette to do . so god yow helpe and al
seyntis

The oth of Scavageours

// j.   E shuln swere that yee shul over see diligently
    y   the pavymentȝ withyn your warde beyng
           wele and Rightwisly Repaired and nat enhaunsed to
nuysaunce of neighburghs and that the Chemynies streatis and
lanes bien cleene of Rubous fyme and of al manᵒ of ordure
for the honeste of the Citee And that al Chemynyes fourneys
Ovenes and herthes bien of stone and sufficient defensable
agenst the pil of fuyre //

// ij.   And if ye fynde any thyng to the contrarie yee shuln shewe
it to yowr Alderman so that the Alderman may ordeigne for
amendement of that And that ye leve nat so god yow help and
al seyntis

The oth of Bedils

           E shuln swere that wele and honestly yee shul   138
                                               Cxxxviij
                                               // j.

    y   kepe the warde of whiche ye bien Bedils and þᵗ
           yee suffre noman Reve ne Robbe nor of evel covigne
or felawship ne hukstrie of Ale ne womman that holdith bordel
house or other womman comune esclaunderes of evil fame and
nuysaunt of lif to dwelle or abide in the same warde that yee
anon shewe thê of suche to the Alderman to that ende that he
do put hem out withyn .xv. daies //

And if the Alderman do nat so yee to do anon after the .xv.   // ij.
daies the Maire to wite //

And if any make affray or draw swerd or knyf or other armure // iij.
yee to maken it knowen to the Chambrelayn of the Citee or to
the Shereves so that they ~~make~~ mown levie bi their ſiauntis
of suche mysdoers this that is to be don and ordeigned for the
pees of our lord the kyng //

And also yee shul Retoᵗne in to the hustynges and bifore   // iiij.
Shereves and Coronsᵍ goode men and triewe vpon enquestes
and nat men suspect of mayntenᵃnce of parties //

And the Retourn that yee make ye shuln shewe to youre   *// v.*
Alderman .ij. or .iiij. bifore the hustyng that he may over see
if yowre Retourne be sufficient or nat And þᵗ yee ne knowe
pultrie nor other smal vitaile cornes ne graynes ne brede to
be Received in pʳve place ne to be sold in hidlis but that yee
warne the Maire and the Shereves of that //
Ne that ye bere non Office in cristen Court duryng thuse and   *// vj.*
office of Bedelrye and althynges that appenden to your office
weele and triewely yee shuln do so god yow help and al
seyntis /

        lso ordeigned it is that al tho that wiln   *. to fynd*
   a playne and pleate bifore the Maire bi bille   *sewʳte*
        shuln fynde plegge or borowes to pursue their billes   *before the*
and than the Maire or the Recorder shal sette his signet to the   *mayr to*
biłł and do a Clerc to write vpon the bil the day that it was   *pʳsue their*
entred and accept and after deliv̇ the biłł to sum ſiaunt for to   *bylle // j. n*
ſve it and the Maire doo

138v   shal over that hasty Right from day to other without any delay
after the vsages and customs of the Citee or lawe Marchaunt
and that al thissues and the amꝰciamentis that fallen of suche
manꝰ of billes shuln be levied to ~~thoffi~~ thuse of the Shereves bi
their Ministres And that the Shereves han in the Court of the
Maire from day to other redy in the handis of a Clerk and a
ſiaunt to entre the plees vicountals that ther shuln be pleated
and to Receive thamꝰciamentis of the same in the forme that
ensueth //

// ij.   That is to wite that of evy pleynt of dette wherof the somme
amountith to þᵉ smᵃ of .xl.ˢ or above thamꝰciament shalbe .xij.ᵈ
and no lasse And if the soṁ be withyn .xl.ˢ the amꝰciament
shalbe .iiij.ᵈ and nomore Savyng alwey to the ſiauntis of the
Maire and of the Chambre .iiij.ᵈ for their fees of hym that shal
Recouv̇e // But the ſiauntȝ ne their yemen ne shul take nothyng
of the defendaunt of no defendaunt for their fee of measne but
of that defendaunt that is acquite by nonsuyte of pleintief or
in other maner whiche defendaunt so quit shal paie .iiij.ᵈ to
the ſgeauntȝ for their fee and the pleintief shalbe amꝰcied as it
is aforsaide after the some that the pleintief demaundiþ in his
bille for dette and for damages //

// iij.   And also savyng the half of fynes of affraies and of bloode
shed to thuse of the comune and that oþꝰ half to thuse of the
Shereve as after more playnly shalbe declared And if the
Shereves ne han nat ther clerkis to entre suche plees . but that
it behoviþ to clerkes of the chambre to entre the same plees in
their defaute that than thamꝰciamentis shuln be levied to thuse
of thê of the chambre //

// iiij. And that no bil bitwene ptie and partie shalbe ſved bi any
ſiaunt if he ne have the signet pleggis and Remembraunce of
the day as it is abovesaide And that

56

ther be no bil abate for defaute of forme if he have matier
sufficient but be he ther anon amended

// v.

And do the Maire due and hastief execucioun̄ to al tho as
wele straung˚s as . Denisyns that so wiln hem silf fresshly
pleate bi the Statute of Smythfield //

But if thei ne playnen nat freshly withyn .viij. daies after their
bargayne made that thei wiln be at the comune lawe of the
Citee thei han lost thauᵃntage of that estatute

// vj.

       lso that eꝰy quarter of the yeere be it cried thurgℏ the
 a   Citee that if any man feeliℏ hym silf agreved and
       wil compleyne vpon the Shereves Clerkes ꝼiauntȝ
Bailliefs Bedilfs . Conestables . jailers or other mynister of
Newgate yemen of ꝼiauntȝ or any other Ministres of any
extorcioun̄ wrong or grevaunce bi hem or bi any of hem don
If he come to the Maire and Aldermen and make his pleynt //
The Maire Recordour and Aldermen shuln don hym Right in
covenable manꝰe and over this to punysṡ the trespassours and
chastise theym after their desert //

And if thei faile to do Right as god defende Shewe he his bille
in thassemble chosen for þᵉ comunes and thei shuln pursuen
for hym to the souꝰaynes to þᵗ end that he have Right and
Reson //

Purveied and forseen that he that playneℏ falsly . vpon any
mynistre and of þis cyte be atteint bi due manꝰe without fauoˣ
don to Ministre vpon whom he haℏ also playned . than suche
a pleintief and also atteynt shal have the same punyshement as
þᵉ defendᵃunt shuld have if he were atteynt

// j.

.pclamacion
euꝰy qᵃtꝰ
to be
made for
cōplaÿtꝭ
// ij. of the
shryves
clerkꝭ
// iiij.
ꝼiauntꝭ
baylliefꝭ
bedyllꝭ
// iiij.
cōnstabullꝭ
jailers
& other
ministˢ /

Thoffice and the fees of the comune ꝼiaunt of Armes

       lso that the comune ꝼiaunt of armes of the Citee
 a   that otherwise is saide comune Crioˣ be alwey of
       the Maires mayne that for the tyme shalbe . and Redy
at his comaundementȝ as thoother ꝼiauntis bien and shal take
eꝰy yeer of the chambre .lx.ˢ and more if this seeme Resonable
to the ~~Aldermen~~ Auditours of thaccompte of the Chamberlayn
vpon his goode beryng and shal take of eꝰiche of the Aldermen
for his fee the Robes al hoℏ with

// j.

139v

the Clokes in whiche thei bien sworn the day that they take
their charge of their office or other wise .vj.ˢ viij.ᵈ at their
plesure //

// ij.

And shal take also for eꝰy cry that he makiℏ for the citee
~~of~~ of the Shereves .xij.ᵈ and to do þᵗ thei shuln fynden hym
sufficiaunt hors for the honeste of the Citee And he shal take
also of eꝰy testament proclamed in the hustyng and of eꝰy plee
tꝰmyned in the hustyng .iiij.ᵈ for his fee //

// iiij.
nᵃ

And suche a ꝼiaunt shalbe charged bi the comune counsail and
Remoeved whan hem pleasiℏ *Of the squire and ꝼiaunt of the*
Maire

57

// j.

                lso the Maire shal have .ij. other ſiauntȝ at the

    a   lest and a Squier weele Inurisshed and taught þᵗ

                can in al places in this that to that ſuice appenditħ
save the honoᵗ of his lord and of the Citee for to bere his
swerd bifore hym at the propre costes of the Maire Savyng that
eɟiche of hem .iij. shal take .xl.ˢ bi yeere of the Chambre and
nomore for his allowaunce and salary And the saide Squyer
shal take over this of Euᵉy lettre þat shalbe ensea7led with the
seal of the Mairalte .xij.ᵈ sauf of Aldermen

// j.

                lso that in the Chambre bien .iij. ſiauntes and no

    a   mo for to ſve the chambrelayn in tho needis þat

                touchen the chambre whiche shuln be chosen . and

    nᵃ Remoeved bi the comune counsail whan theym pleasiþ And
eche of theym shal take bi yeerᵍ for his ˢᵉˡᵃʳʸ ~~salary~~ of the chamb
.xl.ˢ //

// ij.

And thei shuln departe over that bitwene hem the half of the
sõme that shal a Rise of .xij.ᵈ taken for þᵉ entre of the billis of
fraunchise . and that thei bien . clad of the Maires livere at the
costes of the Chamberlayn .ij. tymes in the yeerᵍ

// j.

                lso if any ſiaunt of the Chamber be founde nec

    a   ligent and nat entendaunt to his office bi the

                witnesse of the Chamberlayne . at the first defaute
shalbe abated .xl.ᵈ of his salary . at the secunde dȷ̄ mᵃrc . and

// ij.

at the thrid tyme .x.ˢ // And it is nat the

entencioun) of the comune counsail that thei bien excused of   140
outrageous mystakynges bi thiese peynes . but aftᵍ the quantite Cxl
of suche trespaces bien they Removed or other wise punysshed
after the discrecioun) of the Côen counsail of the saide Citee

                lso that the Chambrelayn Comune ſiaunt of lawe   // j.

    a   other wise named comune speker and the comune

                Clerk bien chosen bi the Comune counsail of þᵉ saide
Citee and Remoeved whan theym pleasitħ //

And shal take eche of hem for his trauaile of the Chambre bi   // ij.
yeerᵍ .x. l̄ī //

And over this the Comune Clerk shal take the sustynaunce   // iiij.
of his clerkis and of eɟy charter on ther deede and testament
enrolled in the hustyngᵍ .x.ᵈ and of eɟ deede enrolled in the
Rollis of the Maire .ij.ˢ and for eɟy biꝉꝉ of assise of nuysaunce
and intrusioun) and for eɟy precept direct to the Sherevis for
plees of hustyngᵍ and for eɟy biꝉꝉ of Scire facias & de fieri
facias .vj.ᵈ sauf of Aldermen //

And the Chambrelayn shal yeeve up his accompt eɟy yeere   // iiij.
bitwene the festis of seynt Mighe11 and seynt Symon and
Jude Apostelis at the furthest byfore .ij. Aldermen . and .iiij.
comuners the whiche shuln be chosen bi the comune counsail
of the Citee the day of seynt Mathew to take the same accompt
and tho chosen shul lymytte to the Chambrelayn certeyn day at
the whiche he shalbe Redy to yield vp his accompte //

And also the wardeyns of the Brigge shuln yeven vp their   // v.
accompt eṽy yeere in the same man⁹ bifore the same Auditours
or other to that assigned bi the côen counsail

       lso if any demaunde to ỿifie any Record shewe / he   // j.
a   to the Chambrelayn or to the Comune Clerk the
     cause of his demaunde . and if it seeme to the
Chambrelayn or to the comune Clerk Resonable be it shewid
vnto hym by a Clerk sworn to the Chambre and non other
wise and if he wil have a copie . have he it ther for competent
salarie to yeve to hym that shal write it // And   // ij.

140v   what Clerk that otherwise shewith the pʳvite of the Rolles and
Recordes and of this be atteynt . atteyntikely be he punysshed
bi his body and leese his office for ever

// j.   lso the Chamberlayns Clerk shal take in partie
    a   a   for his trauaile the half of the sōme that risith
     of .xij.ᵈ taken for entre of billes of fraunchises and
over that he shal take for his trauaile this that the auditours
of thaccompt of the Chamberlayn hym wil alowe after their
discreciouñ

// j.   lso he that is Maire for the tyme and is sworn .
    a   to the Towne and Thescheatour for his tyme that
     he take suche a Clerk for that office for whom . he wil
aunswere aswel to the kyng as to the Citee in savaciouñ of his
honour and his estate

The oth of the Chambrelayn

// j.   E shul swere that wele and triewly ye shul ſve
    y   the Citee of london in thoffice of Chambrelayn and
     whatsumever and asmoche as ye han in warde or
in kepyng touchyng the Citee saufly to kepe and the consail
of the Citee to concele and huyde The Rightӡ of Orphans in
asmoche as to yow atteyneth to konne and mayntene ne no
Recorde ne mynumentis bi whiche the Cite myght be empeired
to noman ye shul shewe nor delyvere / ne no Recorde þat
conteyneth Right of psone maliciously to concele or denye
ne non accepte to the fraunchice of the saide Citee other wise
than is vpon that in this booke ordeigned and that the londes
tenementis and Rentis appteyneng to the Chambre duely yee
shul susteyne and the profiteӡ of the Citee in asmoche as ye
can after Reason to encresce ne the damages of the saide
Citee yee shuln nat suffre But to your power the distourbers or
otherwise to the Maire and to the counsail of the saide Citee
that for the tyme . beyng ye shal do to wite . and in alother
thynges that to yowre office appendith wele and triewly ye
shulbe . have yow as god yow help and al seyntis

The oth of the Côen ſiaunt of lawe

ʏ E shul swere that wele and triewly yee shall // j.
ſve the Citee of london) in thoffice of comune
ſiaunt . and the lawes . vsages and ffraunchiseȝ of
the saide Citee ye shal kepe and defende withyn the Citee and
withoute after yowr konnyng and power and the Rightes of
orphans to save and mayntene and goode . and lawful counsail
ye shul yeve to althynges towchyng the comune profite of the
same Citee and theyr counsail kepe ne comune damage that ye
knowe to þᵉ Citee but that yee shal distourbe or to the counsail
of the Citee lete hem knowe and do to wite and the comunes
of needis of the Citee at al tymes that yee shalbe Required bi
the Comunes in al placis wher neede shalbe triewly yee shal
shewe and tel and ententiefly pursue for the comune . ꝑfite of
the Citee so yow god help and al seyntis

The oth of the Côen ſiaunt of Armes

ʏ E shul swere that wele and triewly yee shal // j.
ſue the Citee of london) in thoffice of comune
Crioˣ and the lawes vsages and fraunchices of the
saide Citee ye shall kepe and defende withyn þᵉ Citee and
withoute after your konnyng and power and the consail of
the citee ye shal huyd and concele ne the comune damage of
the Citee that ye can to yowre power yee shall distourbe or
to the Ministres or to the counsail of the Citee yee shul do to
wite and the comune needis of the Citee at all tymes whan
yee shalbe Required in al placis ther neede shall be diligently
pursue and in alother thynges that to your office appenden wele
and triewly ye shul behav so god . yow help and al seyntis

The Oth of the Comune Clerk

ʏ E shuln swere that wele and triewly ye shal ſue the // j.
Citee of london in thoffice of the comune Clerk þᵉ
lawes . vsages and fraunchices of the saide Citee ye
shal kepe and defende withyn the Citee and withoute after yoˣ

141v connyng and power and al the plees of hustynges and of
nuysaunce with your diligence ye shal sette that they bien
triewly entred and enRold and non enRollement bi yow ne bi
other without thassent of the Maire and Recordour be made
nor do to be made and yee shalbe obeisaunt to the Maire
Juges and counsail of the Citee and goode . counsail after your
connyng and power in althynges touchyng the gouᵘnaunce of
the Citee and the comune profite of the people yee shul yeeve
and the counsail of the Citee ye shal secretly concele and
kepe and the comune damage to the Cite yee shul nat knowe
ne suffre but that ye shul discovere or as to the Ministres
and to the counsail of the Citee yee shal do to wite . and
whatsumever ye have in warde and kepyng touchyng the Citee
savely yee shal kepe and no Record ne other miunimentis bi

60

whiche the Citee myght be empeired to noman ye shal shewe
ne delivere ne no Recorde þᵗ conteyneth the Right of any
psone maliciously yee shal nat concele nor denye . ne no clerk
hold with yow resident in Court . but suche at your pil yee
will . aunswer for And that thei bien sworn in presence of the
Maire and Aldermen and in alother thynges that to your office
appenden wele and triewly yee shalbe have yow in so god yow
help and al seyntis

The oth of the ffiauntis
of the Maire and of the Chambre

// j.

E shal swere that wele and triewly ye shuln
y   behave yow in youre office and due execucioun⁾
do wherof yee shuln be charged bi the Maire
Aldermen and Chamberlayn and of iugementʒ yolden in
the Maires Court without delay yee do and no fynes ne
amᵒciamentis gretter than suche þᵗ bien conteigned in thestretis
whiche bi the Court to yow shalbe delivered of any psone
poore ne Riche yee levie ne non extorcioun⁾ bi colour of yoᶻ
office to any man

yee shul nat do and in enquestis goode folke and triew yee shal 142
Retoᶻne and no suspect folke ne ₚcure to youre knowyng and Cxlij
the comune profite of the citee in asmoche as yee maynteyne
yee shuln avaunce and to the contrary to yoᶻ power / yee shul
nat accorde and agenst the comune people wele and triewly
conteigne and bihave yow //

And in al other thynges þat to yowre office appenden wele and // ij.
triewly yee shul be have yow so god help yow and al seyntis *!ordo! the
eleccion of*
lso in Right of eleccioun⁾ of a Recordour is and // j.   *the*
a   assented that at al tymes that neede shalbe to *recorder of*
chese a goode man to occupie that office . be a côen *london*
semble made of comuners and comune counsail and ther *made by*
amonges hem in comune to be pesiebly debated delibered and *cōmuns*
entreatid what psone theym seeme most able to that office and *& cōmon*
also most profitable for the Citee // *counsaill*

And whan they bien accorded vpon oo psone . be .ij. Aldermen // ij.
and .iiij. comuners chosen and sent to that psone or other wise
sende they for hym as theym best seemen and do their power
to make hym assente to take that office //

And if he wil nat do it . be ther another chosen and Required // iij.
in maner abovesaide and so from psone to psone ~~til to the
tyme þᵗ the Aldermen bien clad in on sute~~ til that sum wil
Receive it //

And he shal take eⱴy yeere for his fee .xl. lī of the Chamber // iiij.
And at al tymes that þᵉ Aldermen bien clad in oon sute he
shalbe clad of the same sute in pellure and liverey at the costes
of the chamber also And shalbe commensal with the Maire if
the Maire wil as it hath wont to be of auncient tyme //

And over this he shal take of e√y chartre testament writen and // v.
deede enrolled in the hustyng .xx.^d //

And no ^fee fee ne Robe of any foreyn lord nor other he shal // vj.
take brynge ne were duryng his office And non Aldermen
shalbe suche but if it be bi thassent of the comune counsail of
the saide Citee

The oth of the Recordour // j. *the*
        E shal swere that yee shalbe feithful and true *recorders*
oth

142v   to the kyng of Inglond and to his heires . and to the Citee
of london and the fraunchices and vsages of the same Citee
withyn the Citee and withoute after yowe power yee shal
mayntene and the counsail of the saide Citee yee shal nat
discovere and that yee shul nat lette for yitf¹ ne for fauo˟ ne
for ˌpmyse ne for hate that evene lawe and Right yee shal do
to al maner of people aswel to pore as to Riche Denisyn as
straungier that bifore yow shal pleate in plees hustynges and in
alother maner of plees //

// ij.   And that al þe plees that bifore yow shalbe pleated triewly
ye shal Recorde and your diligence sette and oversee . that
the saide plees bien wele and triewly enrolled ne no Right
distroubled And that no iugement ye ne tarie withoute
Resonable encheason //

// iij.   And if yee knowe the Rightes or the profites of the Citee as in
londis tenementis Rentis forprised w^t drawen conceled or hid .
yee shul shewe to the Maire and Aldermen for the Rightes of
the same Citee to save //

// iiij.   And Redily to come at the warnyng of the Maire or Shereves
or of their Ministres . for goode and holsum counsail hem to
yeve for the state of the Citee to kepe and maynten //

// v.   And tendre shalbe to the Rightes of Orphans to save and to
mayntene after the lawes and vsages of the Citee // ne no
yift of any ˌpsone grete ne smal yee shal take if yee trowe
bi youre conscience that this be to yow more soun⏚ sent for
mayntenaunce of sum quarel or for to distrouble or delaie the
Right of any than for any other love or friendship //

// vj.   Ne no fees ne Robes of any foreyn lord ne of nonoþ⁹ ye shul
nat bere were ne take duryng yo˟ office //

// vij.   And al thordynaunces in this booke in al their articles triewly
yee shul susteyne ne to any ordynaunces contrarie to thiese
yee shul nat assente ne iugement to the cont^ary yee shal nat
gyve without assent of the comune counsail of the Citee ne
non extorcioun⏚ to any ˌpsone poore nor Riche bi colour of yo˟
office yee shul nat do //

// viij.   And in alother thynges that to your office appenden to do yee wele and triewly shalbe have yow so god help yow and al 143

seyntis   The eleccioun̅ of Aldermen   Cxliij

        lso in Right eleccioun̅ of Aldermen be everiche   // j.

a   chosen bi the warde wherof he shalbe Alderman

       and be his name presented to þᵉ Maire bi the grettest

partie of the goode men with the Ministres of the same warde

and ther be he Received and take his charge //

And that eᵥ̸y warde that shal be voide of Alderman bi deth or   // ij.

by ᵥ̸ay cause removed of hym that was Alderman . cheese they

another withyn .xv. daies next after this that thei bien warned

bi the Maire of the voidaunce vpon peyne that if the warde

ne be nat assented vpon their eleccioun̅ withyn the saide

.xv. daies than than in their defaute the Maire with advise of

Aldermen shuln charge a goode man for the saide warde to

governe for the tyme that longith //

And if he that shalbe so chosen bi the warde or bi the Maire   // iiij.

refuse þᵉ charge leese his fraunchice to the whiche he shal

never come ageyn without a fyne lymytted bi assent of the

comune counsail of the Citee

     The oth of Aldermen

        E shal swere that wele and triewly yee shul   // j.

a   ſve the kyng and the Citee of london in the

       office of Alderman in the warde of whiche yee be

Alderman chosen and triewly yee shuln entreate and enfoʳme

the people of the same warde of þinges that appenden hem

to do for the garde and kepyng of the Citee and for the pees

in the Citee to mayntene And that the lawes and vsages and

fraunchices of þᵉ saide Citee yee kepe and mayntene withyn

the Citee and withoute after yoʳ connyng and power And þat

yee shalbe tendre of Right of Orphans to save and to mayntene

after the lawes and vsages of the saide Citee //

And that ye shalbe Redy . and Redily come at þᵉ somons and   // ij.

warnyng of the Maire and Ministres of the saide

143v   Citee that for the tyme shuln be for thasises plees and

       iugementȝ hustynges and other nedis of the Citee to be

       emploied if yee ne be for the needis of our lord þᵉ kyng or

       bi other Resonable encheason distroubled And þat goode .

       lawful and triew counsail yee yeve to the thynges touchyng

       the comune profite in the Same Citee ne no yift of any psone

       grete ne smal ye take if yee trowe bi yoʳ conscience that this

       to yow be more soun̅ sent for mayntenaunce of any quarel or

       for to distourbe or delay the Right of any than for other love

       or friendship And al thordynaunces in this booke in al their

       articles triewly yee shul sustene ne to any ordynaunces or

       iugement contrarie to thiese yee shal nat assente without the

       comune counsail of the Citee //

// iij.   And that due execucioun̄ of presentementȝ in yoᵗ wardmote
yee shuln doo and ententiefly pursue ne non extorcioun̄ to any
psone poore ne Riche bi coloᵗ of youre office yee shul doo And
that wele and triewly yee shul be have yow in the saide office
and al other thynges wherof yee shul entᵒmete touchyng the
saide Citee so god yow help and al seyntes

// j.   lso at altymes whan it cometh so to that
      a   the Aldermen bien clad of oon sute that
         the same clothyng be nat yeven nor in nonother manᵉe
aliened withyn .ij. yeer⁹ vpon̄ peyne of .C.ˢ to paie to the
chambre //

// ij.   And if any of hem die withyn the terme his executours shuln
kepe the same clothyng without alienacioun̄ þᵒof made or doon
til to thend of .ij. yeer⁹ vpon̄ the same peyne

// iij.   lso that non Alderman ne do ne make from
      a   hensfurth any eschaunge with another Alderman
         of his warde ne Remoeve from . warde to warde
without thassent of the commune

counsail of the Citee //   144
And that non that is or bifore hath be Alderman or Shereve   Cxliiij
ⁿᵉ shalbe put in enquestis And that no seisyn of londes or   // ij.
tenementis be from hensfurth delivered or hidde But in the
presence of þᵉ Bedil and other goode men of the vynee aboute
And he that takith the ssin̄ shal paie to thuse of the Alderman
.ij.ˢ and to the vse of the Bedil .vj.ᵈ //
And if the ssīn be pʳvely delyvered without presence of þᵉ   // iiij.
Bedil and neyghburghs shal paie double fee to the Aldermâ
and to the Bedil and nevertheles .xx.ˢ to the Chamber But
seisyne of quite Rent or Rent charge or graunt of Reuᵒsioun̄
may weele passe bi deede enrolled without presence of Bedil
or other as in auncient tyme hath bien vsed
           lso that eⱴy Alderman hold his wardemote .   // j.
      a   iiij. tymes in the yeer⁹ . if it be neede but .ij.
         tymes at the lest . in whiche he shal make diligent
inquisicioun̄ of pointes vnder writen and of all manᵉ of
nuysaunces bifore hym presented due and hastief execucioun̄
to his power he shal do vpon peyne to paie .xl.ˢ to the chamber
if he resonably be founde nᵉligent To whiche wardmote
oughten to come altho that holden . houses or petie Chambres
withyn the same warde and . al the ſuauntis of .xv. yeer⁹ and
more outake appᵒntices and ther shuln altho whiche ne wern
nat bifore that tyme sworn in that warde put in freplegge nat
withstandyng that thei wern Received to that in an other warde
wher thei han dwelt bifore and sworn . the oth vnder writen //

And that eviche that shall so be Received shal paie for his   // ij.
entre .j.^d And if any be absent shal paie .iiij.^d to the Alderman
if he ne have no Resonable encheason and if he ne be Clerk .
knyght or womman //

And the Alderman ought in his owne ‚ppre psone to over see   // iij.
the nuysaunces . of his warde . and vpon that from oon day
unto op⁹

144v   without any tarieng to make due correccioun if ther ne be any
difficulte or hard matier that hym behovith to put vp bifore the
Maire //

// iiij.   And if he fynde thofficers of the warde lacchies in their office
hym ought to comaunde hem to do bettir . and if he fynde hem
disobedient to chastice hem or ellis anon to shewe it to the
Maire and to pursue over til thei bien resonably chastised after
their deft

The oth of theym that shalbe put in free plegge

// j.   E shuln swere that yee be triewe and feithful
      y   to the kyng of Inglond and to his heire
        kynges and the pees of the kyng yee shuln kepe and
to Ministres of the Citee of london obeye and to arreste
mysdoers and disobedient vnto the pees of the kyng yee
shuln be Redy at al tymes to help the saide Ministres at the
warnyng of the Conestables and Bedils to make wacche and
other charges for . the sauf garde of the saide pees aswel
in Deynsyns as in straungiers and al the pointes in this
wardemote to shewe after yowre power wele and truly to
hold //

// ij.   And if yee knowe any evil covyne or felawship withyn the
warde or in the Citee yee shal discover hem to yor Alderman
and do hym to wite and in alother yee shuln do and saye as
goode and true men yow bere so god yow help and al seyntis

how the wardmote shalbe holde

// j.   lso evy Baker ought to bryng his Mark oones
      a   in the yeere to the wardemote whan he shal
        be of this warned bi the Bedill and ther shal his name
be entred with the figure of his Mark and shal paie at the first
entre of his name and Mark .iiij.^d And at the saide wardemote
shal the Conestables Scavegeours and Bedils be chosen and
Remoeved bi þe goode men of the warde in whiche thei bien
officers after

this that

this that hem semeth neede And that non be chosen in þe saide 145
offices if he be nat free of the Citee . and a triew man and of Cxlv
goode beryng // And if any that is chosen ~~chosen~~ Conestable
or Scavenger refuse to take the charge shal paie .xx.ˢ to the
Chamber without Remyssioun) of that to be had // And the
Alderman ought to make his Clerk openly to Rede in Inglissh
the poyntes that ensuen what places hym ought to arraye bi
the Bedil an enqueste of as goode folke ther present as hym
semyth Resonable the whiche shuln bien charged triewly to
inquire and so shuln the Scavengeours and the Bedil be Joyned
to theym of thenquest for theym to enfoͬme And wele may
be that eͮy Bedil may distreyne wᵗ in his baily for dette to the
mountenͣnce of .v.ˢ // But it is lieful to hym that is distressed
to Replevie þe distres in the Shereves Court if he wil and ther
be it detͣ̓myned

The pointes that shuln bien Rad in ful wardemote the
whiche al the folke of the warde shuln be charged stidefastly
to kepe

Irst be it enquired if the pees of our lord the
f   kyng be lasse in goode kepyng and bi whos
defaute and bi whom it is broken or distroubled And
if any be Resteaunt or hauntyng withyn the warde if he be nat
frepleged and if any that is outlawed or endited of felony be
drawyng thider
a   lso if any make Scote ale or is Receivoͬ or gaderer of
evil felaushippes . and if any be a comune Riotoͬ or baratoͬ or
walkyng bi nyght without light agenst the cry of the Maire
a   lso if any hostiler . Tauͬner . or Brewer holdith his dore
open after the houre lymyt bi the Maire
a   lso if any putour . comune haſdour contectour
mayntenour of quarels . champtour . embrasour of enquestis or
other mysdoer be drawyng withyn the warde
lso if any baude comune strumpet . wiche . Scold

145v   or hukster of ale be abidyng withyn the warde
a   lso if any that wil nat socour Conestables and Ministres
kepyng the pees and arreste mysdoers at hue and crie levied
a   lso if any pish Clerk Ryng Curfew after Curfew Runge at
the Chirches Bowe . Berkyngchirche Seynt Bride and Seynt
Gile without Crepulgate
a   lso if any officer bi coloͬ of his office do extorsioun) to
any or be maynteneng of quarels agenst Right or take cariage
or arreste vitailes . vnduely
a   lso if any hath don agenst the Cry of the Maire in any of
his articles
Articles touchyng the rule of vitailes and vitailers
a   lso if any forstaller of vitailes or of other marchͣundises
comyng to the Citee to be sold be Resteaunt wᵗ in the warde

a   lso if any vitailer selle vitaile nat covenable or noysaunt
for the body of man or more diere than is ,pclamed bi the
Maire

a   lso if any selle wyne or Ale above the p^{r}se ordeigned or
otherwise than bi ful mesure / ensealid or if any selle ale to
hukster for to selle ageyne

a   lso if any selle or bie bi mesure or weight nat ensealid or
bie bi oo mesure and weight and selle bi another

a   lso if any hostiler bake brede withyn his hostrie And if
any baker bake brede white or browne to selle without Mark or
take more than .j.^{d} for bakyng of a bussheħ

Articles touchyng p^{r}prestures and defautes

a   lso if any concele the goodis of Orphans of whiche the
kepyng appteyneth to the Chamber of Guyldhalle

a   lso be it inquired if any make p^{r}prestures withynne the
warde as in wallis palleys . stalles . stulpes . doores of Celiers
accrochyng to hym the comune soile

a   lso if any pentys porche geete be to lowe to the .
disturbaunce of Riders or of carriage

a   lso if any cast dung ordure Robous Trunkes or other   146
nuysaunt thynge bifore his neighburghs doores or if any cast   Cxlvj
water or other liquor out at dore or wyndow bi day or bi nyght

a   lso if any comune wey or comune cours of water be
forclosed stopped or distourbled to noysaunce of the warde and
bi whom it is don

a   lso if any pavement be defectief or to hygħ or to lowe to
the distourbaunce of Riders or of cariage

a   lso if any norishe . swyne . kyne . Oxen . Cow or . Calf or
Mallardes withyn the wallis to the noisaunce of neyghburghs

Articles agenst the pils of fuyre

a   lso if any house be covered otherwise than . witħ tile
stone or leede for pil of fuyre

a   lso if any Chymeney . hertħ or fourneys be pilous or nat
covenable agenst thordynaunce of the Citee for to eschewe pil
of fuyre

a   lso if any Brewer Brewe or any Baker Bake witħ straw or
other thyng pilous for fuyre

a   lso if any leepre faitour or myghti begger be suffred
withyn the warde

Articles for officers and other þinges nedeful to the warde

a   lso the goode folk of the warde oughten to purveye and
to cheese officers . That is to wite Conestables Scavageours
Aleconners Bedil and Rakier the whiche shuln be sworn bifore
the Alderman of wele and triew doyng their office

a   lso be ther purveied of a stronge hooke of Irn) wiþ cheyne
and cordis and .ij. long laddres for to eschewe þ^e pil of fuyre

a   lso that e↯y house have bifore his dore in tyme of Somer
a vessel beyng ful of water for socour to be had in pil of fuyre

146v

a   lso if it be founde bifore the Alderman bi the
p̃sentement of the goode men of the warde of any
comune mysdoers or folke of evil suspeccioun̄ anon
bien thei attached bi their bodies bi the Alderman and the
Shereves or their ꝼiauntis if thei bien nat present But if thei be
present thei shuln do it bi the comaundement of the Alderman
and saufly kepe their bodies and their goodis til that thei han
oportunyte to bryng hem . bifore the Maire and Aldermen
. and ther bien they a Resoned of that thei bien endited and
vpon that p̃sented and tho that mown nat acquite hem silf bien
thei punysshed bi empʳsonement or other punysshement bi
the discreccioun̄ of the Maire and Aldermen if the trespas ne
be nat over violent . but if it be violent that the punisshement
of suche be don bi thadvise of the comune counsail   Of
theleccioun̄ of Shereves

a   lso in Right of eleccioun̄ of Shereves bien the
Maire Recordoᵗ and Aldermen and Comunes
assembled the day of seynt Mathew Apostel in man̄
as it is ordeigned in theleccioun̄ of the Maire // And the Maire
shal cheese first at his frank volunte a goode man freely of the
Citee oon of the Shereves for þᵉ yeere ensuyng for whom he
wil aunswer of the half of the ferme of the Citee to the kyng
due . If he bi the Maire chosen ne be nat sufficient // But if
the Maire cheese bi counsail and assent of the Aldermen they
oughten to aunswere with hym and the choise for the Comunes
bi hem and bi the Maire somoned bi the Maire for that cause
as is bifore declared thei cheesen for the comunes anoþer
Shereve for the whiche Shereve the comunes ought to aunswer
of that other half of the ferme due to the kyng if he be nat
sufficient // And if any contrauˢie a Rise bitwene the comunes
vpon theleccioun̄ be it don as it is ordeigned in tharticle of
eleccioun̄ of þᵉ Maire // And if any of theym that than is
chose to be

Shereve Refusith or hym silf enstraungith so that he is   147
~~Shereve Refusit or hym sil~~ nat redy at the Guyldhalle the   Cxlvij
Even of seynt Mighel next ensuyng at .x. of the Clocke for
to take his charge . that anon be ther levied of his goodis
londis and tenementis of hym that so hym absentith .C. l̄i.
that oon half to thuse of the Chambre . and thatother half
to thuse of hym that shal than so . sodainly be chosen and
charged bi his defaute // And if he the secunde chosen refuse
the charge be al his goodis . londis and tenementis arrestid
in the handis of þᵉ Citee and be he that shalbe chosen and
charged bi that defaute founden of his goodis londis and
tenementis arrestid of al costages touchyng that office //

And thold Shereves shuln . come at .xj. of the clock at the furthest to the Guyldhałł and delivere to the Maire in ful Court the Coket and shuln deliveren also to the Maire at the furthest at the gen͛al Court of the Maire that shalbe holden after the feste of þ^{e} Epiphany al the Recordes of plees touchyng frank ten̄tʒ pleated bifore hem in their tyme . wit̄h alother Remembraunce touchyng the Recovers of any ꝑsone vpon peyne of .C. ^{s}. of eche of theym to be levied and to paie to thuse of the . Chamber . that to do the Maire hem warnyt̄h at the day þ^{t} thei shuln be charged // Than the Maire shal delivere the Coket to the same Shereve that hym . silf hat̄h chosen and the Recordis to the Chambrelayn saufly for to kepe and anon be the ne^{we} chosen charged in the fo͛me that ensuet̄h

Thot̄h of the Shereves

Y E shuln swere that yee shuln be feithful and triewe to our lord the kyng and to his heires kynges and the fraunchice of the Citee of london̄ yee shul save and mayntene withyn the Citee and w^{t} out after your power . and that yee be obeisaunt vnto the Maire that for the tyme shalbe and tho that shuln be arrested bi the Maire and Aldermen yee shuln sende to oon of yo͛ Compto͛s saufly to be kept ne yee shuln lete non

147v to maynp^{r}se without thassent of the Maire or of that Alderman and at Resonable comaundement of the Maire ye shulln be obedient and that yee wele and triewly kepe the Countees and Shuyres of london and Middilsexꝰ // And thoffices . that to the same Shires apperteynen to do wele and triewly . yee shuln doo after yowre connyng and power . And that yee do Right aswel to poore as to Riche without any extorsioun̄ doyng to any ꝑsone bi colo͛ of yo͛ office And that no gode custom yee abate . ne non evil yee levie or a Reise And that thassises of brede and Ale and alother assises that to yow apperteynen withyn the fraunchice of the Citee and without wele and triewly yee shuln kepe and do to be kept // And that the iugementes and execuciouns of your court ye tarie nat without resonable encheasoun̄ . ne no Right yee distrouble // And that the writtis that shuln come to yow touchyng thestate and the fraunchice of the Citee . yee Retourne nat afore that yee have shewed hem to the Maire and Aldermen that for the tyme shuln bien and to the counsail of the saide Citee if neede be . and that of hem yee have avisement . and that yee shalbe Redy at Resonable warnyng of the Maire for the pees and thestate of the Citee to be kept and mayntened // And that no yift of any ꝑsone lasse ne more ye take if ye trowe bi your conscience that this be to yow more Rather sent for mayntenaunce of any quarel or for to distourbe or delay the Right of any man þan for any other love or frienchip // And al thordynaunces in this booke in al their articles triewly yee shuln susteyne ne to any ordynaunces or iugementis contrarie to this without

the comune counseil of the Citee ye shul nat assent And that
the Shyre of Middilsex⁹ ne the kepyng of the jail of Newgate
yee shuln nat leete to ferme . and that alother thynges that
apperteynen to your office and the kepyng of the saide Shyres
truly yee shuln do bi yow and bi yowres // And the saide

Citee ye shuln kepe from damage after yoͬ konnyng and   148
power // And the half of fynes of fraies of bloode shed Risyng   Cxlviij
in your tyme to the Chambrelayn truly . yee shuln delivere
or do to be delyvered // And that . yee han nomo than .iiij.
ſiauntis and that wele and . triewly yee shuln be have yow
in the saide office and alother thynges wherof yee entremeten
touchyng the saide Citee so god yow help and al seyntis
      Nd anon aftir this that the Shereves bien sworn
a   al their Ministres of office Clerkes . ſiauntis
    and their yomen Bailiefs of Custumes . and of
Middilsex⁹ . the jailer of Newgate and his Clerk shuln be sworn
and eveiche after this that appendith to thestate that he holdith
natwithstandyng any ooth bifore made to their Maisters //
And he that Refusith the ooth be he foriuged of al offices for
that yeere // And he that cometh nat at that day for to take
the charge bifore the saide Maire and Aldermen . shal leese
al offices for þat yeere // And non of the Shereves ne shal nat
have mo þan .iiij. ſiauntis . But lasse if it may be suffred to do
execucioun) to the needis of the people

Thoth of the vnder Shereves . and of al the Clerkis of Sherevis
    E shuln swer that weel and triewly yee shuln
y   ſve your Maisters that bien chosen Shereves
    of london and of Middilsex⁹ for the yeere to com And
that yee lette nat for yift ne for fauoͬ . for promyse ne for hate
that even lawe yee shuln doo and Right to almaṅ⁹ of people
aswel to pore as to Riche to deynsyn as to straungier that
beforn yow shuln pleate wᵗ out mayntenaunce makyng of any
quarel // And that yee ne suffre to your power any folke to be
somoned in enquestis nor in juries that bien nat goode true and
lawful . and nat of affynite ne ˌpcured bi partie And that al the
plees that bifore yow shalbe pleated truly

148v   yee shuln Recorde and sette yowr diligence in surview and
oversee that the saide plees bien ~~and~~ wele and triewly entred
and enrolled ne no Right distroubled ne extorsioun) to any
psone bi colour of your office ne of the office of your Maisters
yee shuln do // And that no iugement be taried without
Resonable encheason And also the fraunchice of the saide
Citee yee kepe and mayntene to yoͬ power and ye shuln be
obedient to the Maire and to the juges of the same Citee and
the comune profite of þᵉ people whan ye shuln be Required
theym counsail yee . shuln yeeve and concele and amͦcy
noman higher þan it is ordeigned bi the comune counsail of
the Citee and the fynes of affraies and of bloode shedyng wᵗ

oute any concelement with the Chambrelayn truly to accompt
in maner had and ordeigned // And that yee suffre nat your
fermers to take any other custumes þat bien nat due and
Resonable and of auncient tyme vsed in the saide Citee //
And that the writtis that comen to yow touchyng thestate and
the fraunchice of the Citee yee shuln nat Return afore this
that yee han shewed hem bifore the Maire and Aldermen that
for the tyme shul bien and that of theym yee han avisement
and thissues fynes and amͨciamentis that comen to yow vnder
grene wex or the pipe triewly ye shuln levie and no pcel of
that encres and thoo that han bien paied triewly discharge and
another tyme nat aske ne demaunde And that yee charge the
yomen of ʄiauntis that ʄuen for to take cariage . in the Citee
that thei take nomore to cariage than ought to be take ne that
thei ne greve nat the people comyng to the Citee with their
vitailes bi wey of cariage for to have of theym // And that no
jugement agenst any ordynaunce made bi the Maire Aldermen
and comune counsail of the Citee yee . shal nat yielde . if it be
nat bi hem out or amended

And that in thiese thynges and in alother touchyng your office   149
weele and triewly yee shuln be have yow and bere yow so god   Cxlix
yow help and al seyntis

Thoth of the Shereves ʄiauntis

      E shuln swere that wele and triewly yee shuln
y   be have yow in youre office and obedient shuln
      be to the Maire and to the juges of the same Citee and
their honour in asmoche as in yow is yee shul save and kepe
and no fynes ne amͨciamentis gretter þan thoo that shuld be
conteigned in thestretis that yee shul be bi the Court delyvered
of any psone poore ne Riche levie ne non extorciouꝩ bi
colour of your office to any yee ne do . and due and diligent
execuciouꝩ of whatsum ever ye shuln be charged bi the
souͤaignes of the Citee . trieuly and without delay ye shuln
pfourme and in enquestes goode men and true . yee shuln
Retourꝩ and nat to your knowyng folke suspect ne ͵pcured
and non execuciouꝩ of for your owne profite yee shuln nat
tarie . and thordynaunces to whiche the comune counsaile of
the saide Citee bien accorded for the pees of our lord the kyng
and for the comune profite of the people to youre connyng and
power yee shuln maŷtene and kepe and agenst the comune
people wele and peasibly yee shuln conteigne and holde yow
so god yow help and al seyntis

Thoth of ʃiauntis yomen
      E shuln swere that yee shuln be obedient
y   to the Maire and to the souᵉaignes of þᵉ Citee
      and bi coloʳ of yoʳ office yee do non extorcioñ and
that yee take nomore than shalbe neede . ne that yee greve
the people comyng to the Citee witĥ their vitailes bi wey of
Cariage for to have of þᵍ goodis and that the punysshement of
jugementis wherof yee shuln be charged bi youre soveraignes
in goode manᵍ and Rightwis without grucche or warnyng yee
shuln

149v   to culpable in pʳve and apert // And in alother yee shal do and
sey as goode and triew men yow bere so god . yow help and
al seyntis
      lso the same day after Mete thold Shereves and
a   the newe assembled to guyder shuln gon to
      the pʳsone of Newate and ther the newe Shereves
shuln Receive al the pʳsons and pʳsounᵉs bi endenture made
bitwene hem and thold Shereves and ther to sette in sauf garde
and kepyng at their pil wiþ out letyng the jaile to ferme // And
be it don to . wite that al the profites comyng of any customes
. or Bailwikes apparteyneng to the Shereves of londoñ and
Middilsex above the houre of noone the Even of seynt Mighel
abouesaide shuln be to the newe Shereves and bifore the houre
of noone to thold
      lso that no Shereve from hensfurth take fyne
a   of Baker ne of Brewer above that is ordeigned
      to theym for to take // And if any Shereve do and of
this be atteynt shal paie for eѵy peny so . taken or Resceived
.xij.ᵈ. to the Chambre
      lso if it come or happe whiche god defende þat
a   any Shereve or their Ministres han an especial
      comaundement bi the Maire or Aldermen for to
parfourme any neede touchyng the Citee and suche a Shereve
or his Ministres ne wil nat do it anon be that Shereve or the
Ministre warned to come bifore þᵉ Maire and Aldermen and
the comune counsaile of the Citee to aunswer wherfor he hatĥ
nat don this that hym was comaunded // And if he come nat
at the day hym assigned or if he come and yeve no resonable
aunswer ne shewe resonable excusacioñ be he put out of
his office and another enstablisshed in his . place // And if the
defaute be founde in the Minister of the Shereve be he put out
of his offices and foriuged of al other offices to have after in
the saide Citee

for ever without Restitucioun̄) // And also that þᵉ Maire   150
Shereve ne Alderman Clerkis of Sherevis ne of þᵉ chamber   Cl.
ſiaunt ne Bedil ne yoman of ſiaunt ne Portours of Countours
ne officers of Newgate ne their vadletȝ yomen or ſuauntis
from hensfurth ne brewe nat by hem silf ne bi other to selle ne
Bachouse hold ne Cart huyre . ne of no vitail bien Regratours
ne huksters of ale ne partens⁹ with hem // And who that this ne
. wil nat swere . or agenst this ordynaunce shal come be he put
out of his office for ever

             lso that the Shereves or their Clerkis for hem
a   .ij. tymes in the yeer⁹ That is to wite at the
             feste of Ester and seynt Mighel shuln accompt with
the Chambrelayn triewly and without any concelement or
huydyng of fynes . of affraies of bloode shedyng and shuln
delyvere holl vnto the Chamblayn the half of the money
Risyng of that withoute any thyng withholden . and to hold
with hem thatoþ⁹ half for their travaile

             lso that the Shereves shuln delivern the plees
a   of dette . trespas . covenaunt . detenue . and accompt
             pendaunt or hangyîg bifore hem . or bitwene foreyn
and foreyn or bitwene foreyn and Deniȝen from day to other
without any delay and þis aswel after Mete at their Comptours
as bifore hem atte Guyldhalle if it be nat pleated that shalbe
tᵉᵐmyned bi enqueste so alwey that if the foreyns ne bien nat
contynuanly Resteaunt or abidyng withyn þᵉ frᵃunchice of the
Citee . and thei that bien Resteaunt withyn the Citee han thei
issue of their plees as han frank and free Denisyns // And if
oon suche foreyn be abidyng or contynuanly Resteaunt withyn
the fraunchise wage his lawe he shal make his lawe bi his sixt
hand as don thiese frank and free Denisyns // And it is . don to
wite that eⱴy foreyn defendaunt nat Reste

150v   aunt nor abidyng that is Resceived to make his lawe bi his
hande soole and aloone . he shalbe sworn in þᵉ court and
furthermore he shal make the same ooth in .vj. pissh Chirches
after thauncient vsages if the pleintief wil demaunde it //
And be no Capias awarded agenst the Denisyn defendaunt
. but if it be witnessed bi the ſiaunt that he ne hath wherof
to be distressed withyn the fraunchice wher that the pleintief
wil swere or that witnesse be bi .ij. goode neighburghs þᵗ
the defendaunt be futief But agenst the foreyin defendaunt
be alwey Capias awarded anon if þᵉ pleintief ne wil at his
pil certifie to the Court of sufficient forein distresse // And
if the Shereve vndershereve . or his Clerk ne wil nat awarde
the Capias anon to take the bodie of suche a forein or
thattachement vpon his goodis at the Request of the partie that
is frᵃunk and free of the Citee the Shereve shal make gree to
þᵉ pleintief of his damages of whiche he hath in ronne bi the

73

defaute of suche awarde of Capias or of attachement in cas
that the defendaunt this ensue . out of the fraunchice after the
discrecioun̄ and advise of the Maire Aldermen and comune
Counsail

        lso if any free man of the Citee hold his .

a   lawe in Court of Record as a forein for to
        eschape bi his hand soole or aloone leese he his
fraunchice to whiche he shal never come ageyn without fyn
made bi thadvise of the Maire and the comune counsail vpon
whiche be the Chambrelayn warned to do execucioun̄

        lso if any womman covert of husbond vse

a   any craft bi hir silf bi the whiche she .
        is vsed to bie and bargayne vitailes and other
Marchaundise that appendith to that craft and hir husbond
and she bien empleated for thyng that she so hath bought and
bargayned and the hus

bond ne wil nat appiere in Court to aunswere in that cas   151
the wif and takith issue and iugement in man⁹ as if she   Clj.
were soole // And in cas that the . pleintief wil sue bi forein
attachement have he execucioun̄ of al the goodis of the
husbond founden withyn the fraunchice of the Citee

        lso if any have ꝓfred his lawe and after .

a   makith defaute of his lawe to make be it
        anon iugement yolden without any taryeng the
presentence of the pleintief and over that do due execucioun̄
vpon hym and his Maynpnours . And if the pleintief make
defaute be he anon nonsute and lese his pleinte

        lso if any defendaunt in plee of dette . trespas

a   of Accompt . detenue . or of couenaunt made
        withyn the fraunchice of londoñ and the defendaunt
puttith bifore an acquitaunce made in the cuntrey ther wher the
contract was nat made ne there or wher the Court ne may nat
have conysaunce ne knowlache . be it holden for nought // But
go they to iugement nat withstandyng that if the defendᵃunt ne
can nat have any thyng to say with this that . the pleintief in
Court of the Maire make his oth bi due examynacioun̄ whiche
that acquitaunce ne was never his deede

        lso that Executour shal aunswer for his .

a   Testatour of thyng don withyn þᵉ fraunchice
        in man⁹e that ensueth // That is to wite that
thexecutour shal swere with as many psones as the Court shal
seeme Resonable that for non evidence that he . hath . herd .
seen . ne founde ne bi nonoþ⁹ wey to his knowlache was holde
in the demaunde

        lso that no panel be . from hensfurth arraied

a   to be Reto³ned bitwene partie and
        partie withyn the fraunchice bifore justic⁹

151v Maire Shereves or any chargeable matier . but in p̄sence and
bi thadvise of the Maire Recordour and .ij. Aldermen named
of the Maire without ꝑcurement of partie . and oon of the
Shereves at the lest if any of the parties it demaunde // And
that panel so bi hem arraied be . somoned and nonother and
that same forme be holde of . xij . viij . and . vj . tales from
hensfurth if thei bien at seynt Martyn the graund bifore justice
of Nisi . Prius as of alother enquestis taken in the Citee of
london bifore Maire or Shereves aswel for the kyng as bitwene
partie and partie bien thei taken of goode folk triewe sufficient
and nat suspecious // And also the Maire and the Recordour
shuln oversee and make amendes if neede be of the panels
Retourned in hustyng bi the Bedil if any of the parties it
demaunde as of other enquestes // And if thiese enpaneld ne
come nat in Court and aunswere for their names at the first day
bien thei am̄cied and at þe secunde day double and bien thei
distressed agenst the .iij. day bi al their goodis

a lso that in no Court withyn the Citee bifore
Maire or Shereves be any iugement taried .
above the thrid Court next after this the plee bi
comen in iugement if the matier ne be nat openly . knowen
for if dificulte that bihovith of force to have more lenger
deliberacioun̄)

a lso that al maner of men that pleaten for dettis
Recoūed that thei han after theyr Recover
their damages adiuged to hem bi the Court or bi
thenquest // And that the dettour have enp̄rsonement til gree be
made to the partie pleintief aswel of his damages so to hym
// adiuged as of the p̄rncipal dette But if the pleintief shewe
obligacioun̄) to hym made bi the defendaunt and the defendaunt
falsly ageyne saith it and vpon that he is convict . bien the
damages adiuged after the tyme past of paiement bi the

advise of the saide Court and have he enp̄rsonement after the   152
comune lawe   Clij.

a lso that no pleintief be arted any thyng
to paie for thentre of his pleint in plee psonel
and that the pleintief be take in Court with his
attorney for hym to pursue his pleint wᵗ out havyng assoigne
vpon peyne to be a nonsute // And that alwey be it entred
in the Rolle the day þᵗ any makith his entre of his pleinte
or other wise be it hold for nought So that it may be knowe
who is the first pleintief in cas wher bien made many foreyn
attachementis // And if it happen that in oon Rolle bien many
pleintis vpon oon psone that pleint that is first writen in the
Rolle shalbe holde for the first // But it is to wite that he
atte whos sute the defendaunt be first arrested shal have first
execucioun̄) of his pleint // Natwithstandyng that another had
his pleint bifore hym if it be nat in cas that oon be arrested bi
his body at the suyte of a pleintief and after cometh another

pleintief and takith attachement vpon certein goodis of the
same defendaunt withyn the fraunchice And than shal the .
secunde pleintief have first execucioun) of the goodis of the
defendaunt if thei bien sufficient to make asseth to hym and
to the first pleintief // And if thei bien nat sufficient but only
for the secunde pleintief at whos suyte thei wern arrested have
he thexecucioun) of hem And the first pleintief hold hym to
the body of the defendaunt that is arrested bi his suyte // And
in the man⁹ be it don of many attachementis made vpon dyus⁹
goodis of oon defendaunt at the suyte of many pleintiefs And
that the Clerkis of the Shereves entren al the plees pleated
// bifore hem in Rollis if the ꝑtie pleintief it demande And
alwey see the Shereve that he have the defendaunt þᵗ is arrested
bi his body Redy til the quarel be fully endid

152v   and fynisshed vpon pil to aunswer to the pleintief of as moche
           as it semeth ⱬay semblable that he ought to have Recou⁹ed
the costɇ agenst the defendaunt if he had be present
&   lso if any make his pleint agenst another and
Damagɇ   a   his accioun) be tried and founde fals bi due ꝑces
to be   be the damages adiuged to the partie defendaunt bi
jugid   the discrecioun) of the Court // havyng Regard to the trauailes
to the   spenses and Costages that he hath hadde and suffred bi that
defendant cause
                     lso if it happen any in the Court make pleintȝ
           a   oon agenst another and the partie defendᵃunt
                     saith that the pleint is nat triewe and vp on this he
puttith hym silf vpon thooth of þᵉ pleintif to make anoth with
his owne hand aloone and the pleintief wil nat swere that his
accioun) is triewe than be the partie defendaunt adiuged to go
quite and the pleintief be he anⁱcied // And the same lawe hath
the partie defendaunt in that cas if the pleintief profre hym to
swere
                     lso if after iugement yolden afore that
           a   execucioun) be don the defendaunt pᵌchasith
                     a writ of erroᵌ to do come the Record bifore the Maire
or bifore justices bi whiche it be hovith that thexecucioun) of
iugement be put vp in delay of the Recover of the pleintief
in suche cas bien the goodis of hym of the first defendaunt
arrested founden withyn the fraunchice til to the value of this
that was adiuged and of the damages and of þᵉ anⁱciamentis
attached and arrested saufly and . surely to be kept duryng the
plee of erroᵌ so that thexcucioun) of the first iugement may be
in due . manⁱe made and don So also be that the first iugement
be affermed bi the saide Maire or justices So alwey that the
bodie of the first defendaunt . ne is nat in pᵗson bi the first
iugement But it is

lieful to the first defendaunt to fynde suerte for þe goodis   153
abovesaide if he wil // And that no man free of the Citee sue   Cliij.
writ to do come Record and processe fro the Citee to seynt
Martyn the graund bi fore justices bifore that he hath shewed
his grevaunces to the Maire and Aldermen and that bi hem
bien the matiers examyned and the mystakynges bi hem
Redressed if þey mown do it and if thei wiln don it without
long taryeng of partie vpon peyne to leese the fraunchice for
ever and neuᵒtheles to paie to the saide Citee .x. lī. But if the
Maire and Aldermen ne mown nat ne wiln nat Redresse the
mystakynges without long tarieng have he his sute fresshly
bifore the justices at seynt Martyn withoute Empechement
of any // And that no free man of the Citee tarie . tarie no
nother freman in plee out of the Citee of this þᵗ duely may be
termyned duely bifore the juges of the . same Citee if he ne
have nat licence of the Maire and Aldermen for Resonable
cause vpon peyne to leese his . fraunchice // To whiche he
shal never come ageyn wᵗ out fyne made to the Chambre bi
discreciouñ) of the Maire Aldermen and Comune Counsail of
the saide Citee

           lso that the Shereves of the Citee shuln holde thassises   *nota for the*
  a   of novel disseisyne from vtas in to vtas and   *shryves &*
           thassisses of mort dauncestre from quindene in to   *coronir of*
quindene // And that the Shereves and the Coroner ne bien nat   *london .*
absent for voluntarie taryeng of the lawe to do to the parties
vpon peyne of eche of hem .C.ˢ at the lest to paie to the
Chambre

           lso that the Shereves ne lete nat to ferme the .
  a   Counte of Middilsexᵍ in no manᵍ but be it in þᵍ
           propre warde bi their depute so that the people of the
saide Counte and Shire of Middilsexᵍ bien treated and gouᵒned
in due manᵍ as the lawe Requirith without extorciouñ) don
to any

           lso that the saide Shereves ne lete nat þe jaile

153v   of newgate to ferme . but that they sette ther a man sufficient
and of goode fame to kepe the saide jaile in due maner without
any thyng of hym to take for the same garde bi Covenaunt
made prevy or apert // And that the jailer that ther bi the saide
. Shereves shalbe deputed . be he sworn bifore þe Maire and
Aldermen . that he ne nonother for hym ne shal take fyne ne
extorciouñ) of any pʳsoner for settyng on or takyng of Irns and
fetres to take extorciouns of any pʳsoner // But it shalbe lieful
to the saide jailer to take of eⱴy psone that shalbe . delivered
.iiij.ᵈ for his fee as of auncient tyme hath bien vsed // Sauf
that he take nothyng of any man at his entre nor issue sodainly
bi comaundement of the Maire and Aldermen without other
proces // And if it be founde that he do extorciouñ) to any be

he put out of his office and punysshed after the discrecioun of
the Maire Aldermen and comune counsail of the Citee

a   lso that the yomen of ſiauntis that taken
cariage ne taken no mo of Cartes ne of hors
than shalbe neede and thiese of Cartis and hors that
bien to huyre and nat of poore folke that bryngen vitailes and
other marchaundices to þe Citee sparyng Cartis and hors that
bien huyred for singulier profite vpon peyne of to be foriuged
of his office for ever

a   lso that eẏiche that hath huyred any londis
or tenementis of Denȝyn or of foreyn w^t in
the fraunchice of the Citee without especialte therof
had to certeyne terme or to terme of lif and be it in the volunte
and wil of the partie of þat if the Rent be lasse than .xl.^{s} bi
yeere that he warn the lord a quarter bifore at the best // And if
þe value of the Rent that extendith above .xl.^{s} bi yeer^9 than the
lord shalbe warned half a yeer^9 bifore // And if

the tenaunt faile in suche warnynges than he shalbe hold to the 154
lord for the Rent of a quarter or half yeer^9 after the value of   Cliiij.
the yeerely Rent as it is above . saide . or other wise he shal
ordeigne to the lord a sufficient tenaunt for thoo termes // And
the ~~tena~~ lord shal make the same warnyng vnto the tenaunt
at al tymes that hym pleasith to have ageyn the londis or
tenementis in his owne hande for to do his owne wil // And
if the tenaunt have especialte bi deede to terme of lif or to
certeyn terme and the lord withyn that terme alien the same
londis and tenementis in fee in that cas the alienacioun ne shal
distrouble the tenaunt to Receive his terme . but if the tenaunt
ne have non especialte bi deede than the purchasour may do
his owne propre volunte // And if the tenaunt chalenge terme bi
coven^{a}nt made withe lord alonly in presence and audience of
goode men without deede shal have his accioun of covenaunt
agenst the lord and be the purchasour as above at his large //
And if the goodis of the tenaunt bien arrested bi proces at
the suyte of any psone and the same tenaunt be dettour to
the lord of the same house for Rent of that bihynde . than
the lord shalbe ſved of his Rent bifore the first pleintieff //
That is to wite asmoche as the lord wil swere that he is
behynde of the Rente So alwey that the chalenge of the lord
nextende to gretter sōme than the value of the same Rent of
.ij. yeer^9 // And if he have suffred his tenaunt to a gretter sōme
of nounpaiement than the terme of .ij. yeere . be the Remen^{a}nt
at his ṗil of the measne with out preiudice don to hym that
chalengith other dette // But if the tenaunt owe hym other dette
. he shal have his accioun at the comune lawe after þe customs
and vsages of the saide Citee

a   lso if any huyre house londis or tenementis

154v to certein terme or to terme of lif . if he make in any of theym
any aisamentis of tree that bien attached to the principal
tymber of the tenement bi nailes of Irn of the gretnes of .iiij.ᵈ
the C. or gretter or if thei bien attached bi pynnes or nailes
of Tree bi the whiche the principal tymber is pced in part or
thurgh tho aisamentis must dwellen and abide to the lord of
the tenement // And if the tenaunt make herth fourneys with
leede . or Cawdron or Ovene of erth or of stone thiese shuln
abide holl to the lord And the tenaunt at his deptyng shal voide
the house of al the Robous bi hym made . withyn the saide
. house // But it shalbe lieful to the tenaunt to bere awey the
leedes and Caudrons whiche he hath do made there as whan
that he departith so that thei bien nat entred or attacched
withyn the walles of the house be it of stone ᵒʳ of tree without
licence of the lord // And if debate aRise vpon suche Ratynges
bitwene the lord and the tenaunt be the Conestable and the
Scavageours of the warde or sum . of theym and if neede be
. sum masons and Carpientiers . sworn to the Citee juges of
the quarel after the forme vnder writen // And if the tenaunt
feele hym silf a greved bi defaute of couᵗture or other nedeful
sustenaunce of housyng with their apportenaunces ther wher
the lord is holden bi couenaunt for theym to Repaire and to
sustene and the tenaunt hym hath warned or his collectour
of the saide Rent bifore goode men whiche han conysaunce
and knowlache and wiln witnesse that defaute and the lord
ne nonother for hym ne dide amende withyn a moneth after
the warnyng that than ᵗᵒ the tenᵃnt it shalbe lieful to sette
the costages in amendement of that bi the oversight of the
Conestables and Scavengeours of that warde Rebatyng
asmoche of the sõme as he hath so paied at the next termes of
paiement of the Rent
a   lso that al pleaters that pleaten withyn

the Citee shuln pleate in Inglissh and in nonother mañ so that 155
the lay people mown knowe the mañ of þᵉ plees // And that no Clv
pleater attorne from his day ne be nat herde to speke for their
acliauntȝ withyn the barre . in the Court if he be nat comune
ſgeaunt But be thei without the barre without cry or noise
makŷg So that the people of the lawe and the goode men of
. the Citee mown bien herkenyng and heryng in due . maner
of their needis and busynessis that they han to pursue in the
Courtis

The Charter of the ammociouñ and chaunge of Aldermen

Dward bi the grace of god &cᵉ wite yee that among
e   other articles whiche the lord Edward
laate kyng of Inglond our fader the ~~Reigne~~ yeerᵍ of his
Reigne .xj. bi his lettres patentis to the Citeȝeyns of our Citee
of londoñ for the melioraciouñ and amendement of the same
and of the comune weele and profite of al the inhabitauntis
and dwellers in the same and to the same comyng grauntith

79

and confermeth conteyned in the same that of aldermen of
the forsaide Citee from yeer⁹ in to yeer⁹ and namly the day
of seynt Gregory the Pope bien the ammociouns made bi the
Comunalte of the same Citee and to be ammoeved the yeer⁹
folowŷg nat to be ageyn chosen . but in the place of theym
ammoeved bien ther other chosen bi the same wardis of the
whiche the Aldermen wern so ammoeved . as in the same
lettres fully conteigneth vpon whiche for þᵉ ptie of the forsaide
Comunalte bi their peticiouꝺ bifore vs made in oure grete
counsaile now newly don to vs mekely praied and bisought .
as with dyus⁹ contrau⸍sies and oppyniouns bitwene the Alderme
and the Comunalte of that Citee vpon the Ammociouꝺ of
Aldermen for the Synistre and froward intᵖpretacioꝺ of wordis
in the forsaide articles content here therof

155v   wern vpsprungen of so moche that the forsaide Aldermen
affermyng that bi thoo wordis thei bien ammoeved bi þᵉ
Comunalte oughten nat tho aforsaide Aldermen from the office
of Aldermanship to be ammoeved withoute certeyn cause of
the same Aldermen bi the saide Cômunalte don or other for
notarie defaute in the same . founden fforsoth other Citeȝeyns
of the Citee felyng the contrarie long while vpon this bitwene
hem silf contenden and strof wee fouchesauf to take awey
that Article therof bitwene hem al the doubte morefully and
apertly comaunde to be declared // fforsoth wee to the forsaide
supplicaciouꝺ in somoche the gladder as to the same Maire
Aldermen and the comunalte in tranquillite Rest and pees
from hensfurth mown dwelle and a bide fauorably inclyned
that forsaide To the Citeȝeyns and their successours of assent
of the same our counsail in manⁿ vnder folowyng we declare .
that is to say that al and eⱴich Alderman of thelecciouꝺ of the
forsaide eⱴy yeer⁹ imppetuite in the feste of seynt Greory the
Pope from thoffice of his Aldermanship vttirly and precisely
ceesen they and therof al holly bien they ammoeved and to be
ammoeved the next yeere folowyng to the office of Alderman
in no wise bien they ageyn chosen but in place of hem so
ceesed and ammoeved . other discrete of their evene Citeȝeyns
of of goode fame and vnhurt bi the same wardes of þᵉ whiche
thoother so ammoeved bifore wern Aldermen eⱴiche yeere
inppetuite bien thei elect and chosen In witnes of whiche
thyng thiese our lettres patentis strongly . we make witnesse
my silf at Westmynster .xxij. day of Nouember The yeere of
the Reigne of our Realme of Inglond .l. the Reigne for soth of
our Realme of ffraunce .xxxvij.

         he articles of the gouᵘnaunce of fissh and other
t   vitail aswele in the Citee of london as ellis
         wher in our Realme of Inglond ordeigned and statuted
bi our lord the kyng in his parliament holden

at Westmynster . the yeer⁹ of his Reigne .vj. as withynne

       Irst it is ordeigned and statuted that neither in the

f   Citee of london nor in other Citees . Burghs . Towns
       Ports of the See bi al the forsaide Realme any vitailier
from hensfurth any offici judicial . have . excise . nor occupie
in any maner but in townes wher other psones sufficient to this
maner estate may nat be founde // In whiche cas only the same
juge for the tyme whiche stant in office from thexcice of vitail
vnder peyne of forfaiture of the vitails so sold vttirly he ceese
and hym absteyne for hym silf and al his vttirly from the same

       lso it is ordeigned and accorded that whansumever

a   foreyn or alien beyng of the friendship of our
       lord the kyng and comyng withyn the Citee of london
and other Citees Burghs and Townes withyn þe forsaide
Realme aswel withyn fraunchice as withoute . with fissh and
other vitails whosumever he be þ⁹ to dwelle and to their ppre
goodis to ageyn go from hensfurth bien þei in sauf gard and in
especial proteccioun of our forsaide lord the kyng and ther be
it lieful to theym with vigoure and strength of thiese presentis
from hensfurth mown their fissh and aforesaide vitailes
withoute any Impedyment or contradiccioun of whatsumever
to cutte bi fisshes to taile and in parte or in al to Retaile or
in groos as to hym pleasith best to selle and to their owne
profite therof to do whatsumever statutis Charters ordynaunces
. prvelagis or customs made or had to the contrarie nat
withstandyng

       lso it is ordeigned and accorded that whatsumeṿ

a   host aswel at the saide Citee of london and the
       grete townes . Jarnemuth. Scarburgh. Wynchelsey and
Rye as also in whatsumever other townes vpon the cost of
the see and elliswher bi al the forsaide Realme aswel withyn
liberte as withoute from hensfurth vttirly thei ceesen and bien
ammoeved from hem that is to say of noyous and wikke doers
and forstallers and

156v   and in especial bi the kyng it is inhibite to the same that thei
ne non of hem vnder pil that may falle entre mete hym silf no
further imbracyng heryng or oþ⁹ fissh or vitails whatsumever it
be or bi colour of any custom ordynaunce prvilage or Charter
bifore in contrarie þof made or had whiche the tenur of thiese
presentis the Impedymentis bien Reuoked any what prvy
or apert don in bryngen or pcure to be don to any fisshers
Deni3yns or aliens of the ~~friend~~ friendship of our lord the kyng
beyng whiche thei at the lest thei or any of theym arten or
artith to selle his fissh and his vitails . wher whan and to what
and eṿiche psones thei wiln withyn the forsaide Realme for his
lust of voluntarie wil

Nd more over it is inhibite specialy to al and
a   eꝣiche hostes aforsaide that non of hem vnder
    peyne aforsaide entremete hym from hensfurth to bie
selle or Couenaunt any man̄ see fissh or fressh waterfissh to
thuse of any fisshmonger or other Citeȝein of the saide Citee of
london̄)

Nd evene in like wise it is inhibite to al the .
a   fisshmongers and Citeȝeyns of the same Citee of
    london̄) that non of hem vnder the same peyne fer nor
nygh from the same Citee whatsumever see fissh fressh fissh
neither fressh water fissh from hensfurth bie to selle ageyne
in the Citee except fressh Eelis . lucis and pikes whiche aswel
Deniȝyns as foreyns in comune bien and Remaynen to bie or to
selle As longe while Deniȝyns foreyns withynne that Cite Citee
in nowise bien nat letted to selle this man̄ of fissh as often as tho
fisshes bien brought or don to be brought to the forsaide Citee

lso it is ordeigned that whatsumever Maire
a   of london for the tyme beyng amonges other
    thynges from hensfurth be he charged in his at
theschequer of our lord the kyng to make that

he the

he thordyn^ance of ffisshmongers and vitailliers as it is aforesaide 157
withyn his Bailwik he shal holde and do to be holde and of   Clvij.
execucioun̄) he shal do to be kept . duely . al fauour sette
aback // from tyme in to tyme duely he shal demaunde // And
in like maner they shuln be charged from hensfurth in special
. Maires Bailiefs and alother goū̄nours of the Citees . Burghs
and Townes and to this man̄ of vitailliers obteigneng eꝣy wher
~~bifor~~ bi al the saide Realme withyn liberte and withoute ~~vm~~
eꝣiche and singulier of their oothes vp on his newe creacioun̄)
in his office to make // That is say that of this man̄ ordynaunce
asmoche as to þem is and either of hem atteyneth in their
Bailwikes . don to be holden and stidefastly to be kept
In suche a charter of libertes and fraunchises graunted to the
Citeȝeins of london̄) bi henry last kyng of Inglond the .xxvj.
day of Marche the yeer⁹ of his Reigne .lij. conteigneth so

Nd that no Marchaunt or other . go to mete
a   Marchauntis comyng bi lond or bi water w^t
    his Marchaundises and vitailes to bie and to selle
ageyn til they comen to the saide Citee and thei sette ther
marchaundise to saale vpon forfaiture of the thyng so
bought and peyne of emp^rsonement from the whiche he shat
eschape nat without g^ruous chasticement and that nô sette his
marchaundises to sale whiche owen custom til the custom be
levied vpon forfaiture of al the goodis of whiche thei happen
to bryng with hem . other articles in the same chart⁹ content for
vs and our heires of certein causis at the instaunce of the saide
Citeȝeins vttirly we adnulle

ANNOTATED TRANSLATION

[f. 133]

The Prologue of the problem in the new book of the ancient customs and usages in the city of London, compiled and affirmed by the mayor, aldermen and commons of the same city, in the first year of King Richard the second.[1]

The perfection of all policy and the ground of good government dwells and abides upon two things which cannot be separated or parted but should always be held together and maintained: firstly that the wise and righteous governance of the common people should be ordered and modified in rigour and leniency according to current circumstances; secondly that the common people should be reasonable, united and deserving, and loving towards their governors and rulers, fearing them and obeying them. If these two things are well and steadfastly observed by both parties then every city shall be established [...] in tranquillity [...]

[here the page is torn and only a very small section of the text is preserved. There is reference to 'the principal city of the realm' – clearly London – and the names of Nicholas B[rembre, the mayor], [Nicholas] Twyford, Adam of [St. Ive], [William] Walworth, all aldermen, followed presumably by the names of the crafts that were present]

[f. 133v]

Ironmongers, Smiths, Lorimers, Haberdashers, Leathersellers, Masons, Carpenters, Butchers, Cordwainers, Curriers, Tanners, Whitetawyers, Bowyers, Fletchers, Spurriers, Horners, Weavers, Fullers, Dyers, Shearmen, Glovers, Pouchmakers, Founders, Brasiers, Waxchandlers, Tallowchandlers, Hurers, Hatters, Fusters, Joiners, Woodmongers, Turners, Coopers, Jewellers and Paternosterers, or makers of beads, which aforesaid persons wanting to consider the many good articles touching the principal governance of the said city, but that the good customs and ancient usages of the same are compiled in various great books of the same city which require great diligence to search and seek at convenient times, so that the commons of the city cannot consult them

---

[1]   22 June 1377–21 June 1378.

without paying large sums to the appointed officers,[2] have unanimously agreed that all the following articles, to the honour of God [...]

[here the missing portion of the page again breaks the text. There is reference to 'the profit, rest and tranquillity of the said city', 'in name and by consent of all', 'the Holy Evangelist']

[f. 134]

[The Common Council]

[...] always that the greatest crafts may choose no more than six persons, the middle crafts four and the least, two persons, who should dwell, endure and abide for the following year in that Council without swapping unless they are excused by death or another reasonable cause. And if anything is ordained by the mayor and aldermen that touches the commonalty without the assent of those chosen, or the greatest part of them, or at the least twelve of the most qualified crafts, then that ordinance shall be held for naught.[3] And all those so chosen shall be charged by oath in the following manner, that is to say:

The oath of those chosen for the Common Council[4]

I. You shall swear that you will be ready to come when you are summoned for the common council, and you shall give good counsel in accordance with your wisdom and knowledge, and you will not, for any favour, maintain any particular interest against the common profit of the city, saving the reasonable concerns of each craft. And when you have

---

[2]   The 'various great books' would have included the city's Letter-Books dating from the reign of Edward I, the city's custumals, the *Liber de Antiquis Legibus* compiled by Arnald fitz Thedmar c.1274, and the *Liber Horn* and *Liber Custumarum* bequeathed to the city by Andrew Horn in 1328. Access to these volumes was controlled by city officers who charged for their services, see C.M. Barron, *London in the Later Middle Ages* (Oxford, 2004), 181.

[3]   Election of the common council by crafts agreed 27 Nov. 1376, *CLBH*, 37–8. 6 Nov. 1380, considered whether to return to election of the common council by wards and this was agreed 29 Jan. 1384, on the grounds that decisions of the common council had been 'carried by clamour rather than by reason, and sometimes by members who were not qualified to sit', *CLBH*, 156, 227. John Carpenter's explanation for the return to election by the wards was similar: '*Sed stabante ista ordinatione, crevit tumultus in populo, et parvipendebantur majores a minoribus*', *Liber Albus*, 41.

[4]   This version of the oath is almost exactly the same as the French version found in *CLBH*, 41–2, where the common councilman is to come 'unless you have a lawful and reasonable excuse'. 27 May 1377, five men were removed from the common council because they were in the habit of betraying its secrets, *CLBH*, 64. 20 June 1384 a new French version of the oath was agreed: it began with a promise to be faithful to the king and his heirs. The clause 'saving the reasonable concerns of each craft' was removed and a final clause was added 'and what shall have been said in common council you will keep secret', *CLBH*, 240 and LMA, COL/AD/01/008, f. 178 (hereafter LBH). Latin versions of this amended oath are found in *CLBD*, 2, and in *Liber Albus*, 41. A fifteenth-century English version of the oath is found in *CLBD*, 192.

come to the council, you shall not leave without a reasonable excuse or permission of the mayor, nor before the mayor and his fellowship have left. So help you God and all saints.

2. And if any craft fails to return the names of their craft to the mayor on the day that he takes up the mayoralty, the members of that craft shall incur a fine of 6s. 8d. without any redress.

3. And everyone so chosen who fails to come to the Guildhall at any time when they have been warned or summoned, shall pay 2s.[5] And those who fail to appear shall be fined by a sergeant of the Chamber, if their fellowship or fellows cannot excuse their absence in good faith. And each person so chosen is to report yearly to the new mayor of the time.

The days of the Common Council

1. Also every quarter year, or at least once a year, the aldermen and chosen Commons shall assemble to discuss and deal with the needs and business of the city [f. 134v] and on the day that the Commons are assembled no pleas shall be heard between parties in the mayor's court, nor in the sheriffs' courts. Sheriffs who disregard this to be fined £10, for the use of the Chamber, without redress.[6]

2. The first meeting day shall be the first feast day when there is no Husting Court, after the presentation of the new mayor at the king's Exchequer or at the Tower.

3. The day in the next quarter shall be the feast of St. Gregory the Pope [12 March], provided that it is not a Sunday, for on Sundays and Husting days the aldermen are excused from meetings.

4. The day in the next quarter shall be the fourth Wednesday after Easter and the day in the last quarter shall be the third day after the feast of the Translation of St. Thomas of Canterbury [7 July], provided it is not a Sunday or a Husting day. In that case the day shall be the next feast day after that Sunday or Husting.

5. On St. Matthew's day [21 September], when the sheriffs are chosen, the mayor at the time shall always cause to be summoned and assembled, together with some other qualified people at the discretion of the mayor and aldermen, people other than those chosen by the crafts, and these, when they are called by name, should enter the chamber of the common council together with the others who have been elected, and they shall be sworn before the commons to be true and to give their best advice without fraud or malice, paying no regard to the particular interests of

---

[5]   31 July 1384, the fine was raised to 40d., *CLBH*, 240.

[6]   27 Nov. 1376, common council to meet every quarter, *CLBH*, 40; 22 June 1383, common council to meet at least once a quarter. The closing of the courts of the mayor and sheriffs was reiterated, but not the proposed fine for the sheriffs, *CLBH*, 241.

their friends, but concerned only for the common good. If those not chosen by the crafts have not held office in the city as an alderman or sheriff, then they shall say so and be charged according to the oath that they have already taken in the town to say and give counsel as best they can, in the same way and in the same manner that the other commoners who have not held office have been expressly sworn for the selfsame purpose.

And at all times that the commons shall be assembled together with these others chosen for the common good and the needs of the town and paying attention to the time and hour when any serious matter arises in the city. Or if in the assemblies of those chosen, [f. 135] a matter arises about which they may not or cannot agree, then the mayor with the advice of the greater part of the aldermen shall summon further people from the wisest and most qualified commoners of the town, to such number as shall seem necessary to the mayor and aldermen for resolving the matter, so that the said summoned people are together with the elected ones as is aforesaid.

6. And at the least the mayor shall cause to be summoned those elected, at all times that it seems to him to be expedient and necessary to take counsel upon such matters touching upon the common profit or needs of the city.

7. And if it happens that not all those summoned come, nevertheless if the mayor has some people present from each of the twelve most qualified crafts, then the mayor with eight aldermen and those that are present for the commonalty, ought to proceed to deal with the necessary and expedient business, and bring it to a conclusion, unless the matter is so weighty that it cannot be fully dealt with without wider consideration.

8. And all those that are so chosen are to be charged on oath on the same day that their names are returned, if they are present. And if they are not present, they are to be fined, unless excused as above rehearsed, and nevertheless they are to be warned to come on a specified day to take their oath or suffer a double fine.

And if anyone leaves without licence then he is to be fined as if he had been summoned and failed to come.

1. Also, none of those chosen while they occupy that office as common councilmen shall be put on inquests unless it is a plea of land where no others sufficiently qualified can be found. Nor are they to be made tax assessors nor collectors of tallage, nor summoned nor included in common watches, except those when the mayor, sheriffs or aldermen of their wards carry out watches in person.[7]

---

[7]   8 Jan. 1383 and 31 July 1384, this concession reaffirmed, *CLBH*, 209, 241. See also agreed exemption, 9 Aug. 1376, *CLBH*, 44.

2. And if any sheriff returns the names of any who occupy such office, other than is written above, then he himself is liable to the same fine by distraint [compulsory seizure] of the mayor, as that which the party whose name he returned would have paid.

[f. 135v]

The manner of electing the Mayor of London on St. Edward's day [13 October][8]

1. Every year all the aldermen shall assemble at the Guildhall on the feast of the Translation of St. Edward[9] together with those chosen by the Commons and others summoned for that day by the advice of the mayor and aldermen to choose a mayor for the next year in the following way:[10]

Those chosen by the commons and the others expressly summoned for that purpose shall be called by name by a sergeant from a window that is above a flight of stairs going up from the Guildhall into the chamber of the said council, and only those called by name to intermingle in that chamber on that day, upon pain of imprisonment, as shall always be the case when they are assembled for the city council.

2. And the mayor, recorder and aldermen shall remain and stay in one of the ground or lower chambers until the Commons have decided by good deliberation of two persons who seem to all of them, by their oaths, to be qualified and competent to occupy the mayoralty for the coming year.

3. And if controversy should arise among them, some wanting one person and others another, then straight away two of the most qualified commoners, chosen by common assent of all, together with the common sergeant, shall privately ask each person individually to which of the two men under consideration they would more gladly give their assent, and the man with the greater number of supporters shall be taken to be elected.

---

8   On 20 June 1384, the detailed procedure for electing the mayor set out here in paragraphs 1–5 was modified and simplified 'as was anciently accustomed to be done', *CLBH*, 241–2. The procedure set out by John Carpenter is quite different, *Liber Albus*, 20–7.

9   The date of 13 October for the election of the mayor was fixed in 1368, *CLBG*, 198 and n. 2.

10 A royal writ of 1315 restricted attendance at the election of the mayor to those who were summoned, *CLBD*, 24–6; 28 Oct. 1346, decided that the mayor should be elected by men chosen in the wards, *CLBF*, 304; 9 Oct. 1370, royal writ restricted those present at elections of the mayor and sheriffs to those summoned, *CLBG*, 265; 1 Aug. 1376, decided that the new mayor should be elected by men chosen by the different crafts together with the current mayor and aldermen, *CLBH*, 39; 20 June 1384, mayor to be elected by at least sixteen aldermen, members of the common council and others 'more sufficient', *CLBH*, 241; 1386, election of the mayor was restricted to those summoned, *CLBH*, 289; Barron, *London in the Later Middle Ages*, 148–51.

4. And the two commoners and the common sergeant are to be charged on their faith not cause any person to be persuaded or forced with respect to that deed, but to allow each of them to speak freely and from the heart, and they are to report truly which of the two men secured more support.

5. And when they are agreed in the name of God on the two persons, they are firstly to descend to the mayor and aldermen, showing them their choices, and then right away they shall descend into the Guildhall to the other commons, if there be any, and there wait for the mayor and aldermen at the dais of the Husting until they come, and tell them [f. 136] which of the two they have chosen.

6. And whether he who is chosen is present or absent at that time, he is to be ready at the Guildhall by 10 am on the following feast of SS. Simon and Jude [28 October] to take up his charge. And if he fails to appear, the second man who was named with him, shall be sent for and charged with the office on the same day. And the sheriffs shall immediately levy £200 from the goods, lands, rents and tenements within the city franchise belonging to the man who had absented himself, to the use of the man who had had to take his place because of his default, without any remission.[II]

7. And if the second man who was chosen in this way is absent on the feast of SS. Simon and Jude [28 October], he shall pay £200 to the use of the Chamber, and the first man's £200 shall go to the man who is then chosen as mayor because of his default.

Provided always and it is agreed that for five years following his mayoralty, a man shall not be chosen nor forced to serve again as mayor except by his own free will.

1. Also, as at all times, the official assembly shall be the commons, and they shall be assembled and proclaimed in the manner abovesaid.

2. And if any controversies arise and are debated between them touching the matters for which they have been summoned, they are to be resolved in the same manner as in the election of the mayor.

The fines of those that fail to come to the Common Council

1. Also every alderman is to be present in the Guildhall on both the aforesaid feasts [of St. Edward and SS. Simon and Jude] upon pain of paying of 100s.; and those chosen by the commons and summoned for

---

[II]   28 Oct. 1346, decided that a man who was elected as mayor but failed to turn up to take the oath was to be fined 100 marks (£66 13s. 4d.), *CLBF*, 305; 13 Oct. 1368, Walter de Berneye, mercer, failed to turn up to take the oath having been elected mayor and was fined 100 marks which went to Simon de Mordone, stockfishmonger, who took his place, *CLBG*, 234, 240.

that day and who fail to come are to pay 2*s.* to the Chamber unless they have a reasonable and acceptable excuse.

2. And the common sergeant shall provide a written indenture for the chamberlain with the names of those who failed to appear, and the chamberlain shall levy the said fines and shall answer for them in his account. And the common sergeant shall make such a copy on all the six days that have been designated for meetings of the common councils of the city.

[f. 136v]

3. And the mayor shall be charged upon the book to keep and maintain the ordinances in the following manner.

The Oath of the Mayor[12]

1. You shall swear that you will well and truly serve our lord the king in the office of the mayoralty in the city of London, and keep the same city safe and sure to the immediate benefit and profit of the king of England and of his heirs of England, and this you will cause in all things that are appropriate for you to do so. And you will truly observe the king's rights in everything that pertains to the Crown in the city, and you will not assent to damage, nor conceal, nor hide the rights and franchises of the king.

2. And where you know the king's rights to have been withdrawn, you shall make every effort to restore them and, if you cannot do so, then you shall inform the king, or those of his council whom you can be sure will tell the king.

3. And you shall truly and rightly treat those in your bailiwick without committing any extortion on the strength of your office.

4. And you shall do right to everyone, both stranger and denizens, poor and rich as far as you can, and for no high reward, nor for riches, nor for gifts, nor for promised favours, nor for hatred, shall you wrong anyone, nor disturb any rights, nor shall you take anything which might lead to the king losing, or being violated in, his rights.

5. And you shall be solicitous and take care of the rights of orphans, to preserve and maintain them from the Chamber, according to the laws and customs of the city, and not to allow them to be married under age without immediately exacting the prescribed penalties.

---

[12] 1313, earliest version of the mayor's oath in French, *CLBD*, 11 and n. 4, 22–3. This French version is also found in *Liber Albus*, 306. The oath in the Jubilee Book adds the words 'without committing any extortion' to clause 3 and adds an extra clause relating to orphans. There is a fifteenth-century English version of the oath which omits the two additions but adds two new clauses to the original oath, emphasising the responsibility of the mayor for food prices and for true weights and measures in the city, *CLBD*, 34.

And you shall be attentive to all the ordinances in this book, in all their articles, and shall uphold them as far as you can, and not agree to any ordinances or judgements contrary to them without the consent of the common council of the city.

[f. 137]

6. And in all things relating to the mayor of the city you shall well and truly act and behave, so help you God and all saints.

When the General Court of the Mayor shall be held

1. The mayor shall always hold his general court as is customary on the Monday following the feast of Epiphany.[13] At which court the aldermen and sheriffs shall be present and also the officers of every ward unless they have a good excuse, that is to say constables, scavengers and beadles, who shall take up their charge there in the presence of the mayor notwithstanding any charge they may have taken before their alderman.

And if any alderman is absent from the court without reasonable excuse, he shall pay 100s. to the use of the mayor; and any officer who is absent shall pay 2s., and the common sergeant shall make a copy for the chamberlain, as described above.

2. And if any alderman, or other officer at that court, present any trespass committed in their ward against the king's peace, or against any city ordinance, then the culprit is to be immediately distrained to answer, or arrested in person if he has no goods whereby he may be distrained, and the matter resolved in accordance with the laws and customs of the city. The sheriffs shall not release, nor let out on bail such culpable persons without the assent of the mayor and aldermen on pain of paying 100s. to the Chamber.

3. And if any alderman should attempt to support such a malefactor or wrongdoer, he shall on the first occasion pay 20s., and on the second occasion 40s. And if he continues in spite of the fines, he shall be ejected from the office of alderman.

4. And if any officer or anyone else causes anything likewise he shall pay on the first occasion half a mark [6s. 8d.] and on the next occasion one mark [13s. 4d.] and on the third occasion he shall lose the freedom and his office.

---

[13]   6 January.

[f. 137v]

5. And the mayor shall duly cause these and all cases put before him in that court to be executed, without causing any to be delayed.

The Oath of Constables[14]

1. You shall swear that you shall keep the peace of our lord the king well and truly according to your power, and you shall arrest all those who make dissension, riots, quarrels or affrays, so breaking the king's peace, and take him to the house or counter of one of the sheriffs. And if you meet resistance from any such wrongdoer, you shall raise the hue and cry, and pursue them from street to street, and from ward to ward, until they are arrested.

2. And when asked by the scavengers or beadles, you shall search at all times for common people not of the ward, and any faults that you find you shall present to the mayor and officers of the city.

3. And if anyone impedes you in carrying out your office properly, you shall give to the mayor and the council of the city, the name, or names, of those who are obstructing you.

4. And this you shall not overlook, so God you help and all the saints.

The Oath of Scavengers[15]

1. You shall swear that you will diligently oversee the pavements in your ward, ensuring that they are well and properly repaired and not raised to the nuisance of their neighbours, and that the roads, streets and lanes are clear of rubbish, dung and all manner of filth for the well-being of the city. And you shall see that all chimneys, furnaces, ovens and hearths are of stone and built sufficiently strongly against the perils of fire.

And if you find anything to the contrary you shall show it to your alderman, so that he can have it amended.

And this you shall not overlook, so God you help and all saints.

---

[14]   There are no significant differences between this version of the oath and the earlier, and later, French versions, and the later English version, *CLBD*, 10, 192–3, *Liber Albus*, 312; 12 Nov. 1364, decided by the mayor, aldermen and 'good folks' of the city that ward constables were to bring peace-breakers to the sheriffs' counters. They were also, with the beadles, to search houses in their wards for those breaking the assize of food, *CLBG*, 197–8.

[15]   There are no significant differences between this oath and the earlier, and later, French versions, and the later English version, *CLBD*, 10, 192, *Liber Albus*, 313. 12 Nov. 1364 the mayor, aldermen and 'good folks' of the city laid down the duties of scavengers, much as they are set out in this oath, *CLBG*, 198.

The oath of Beadles[16]

[f. 138]

1. You shall swear that you will well and honestly keep the ward of which you are beadles, and that you will not allow any robbers or thieves, or evil gangs or bands, or hucksters [sellers] of ale, or women who keep brothels, or other women who are antisocial and common slanderers of bad reputation, to live or remain in the same ward, but you will promptly show them to the alderman so that he can expel them within fifteen days.

2. And if the alderman fails to do this within fifteen days, you are to inform the mayor.

3. And if any man makes an affray, or draws his sword or knife or other weapon, you are to inform the chamberlain of the city, or the sheriffs, so that they may have such wrongdoers arrested by their sergeants. This is to be done, and is ordained, for the peace of our lord the king.

4. And you shall report to the Husting, and to the sheriffs and coroner, good men and true to serve on inquests, and not men suspected of maintaining parties.

5. And the report that you shall make, you shall show to your alderman two or three [days] before the Husting, so that he may check whether your report is sufficient or not.

And you shall warn the mayor and sheriffs if you know of poultry, or other small victuals, or corn or grain, or bread, being received in hiding places and sold secretly.

6. You shall not hold office in a church court while you hold the office of beadle, and all matters that relate to your office, you shall carry out well and truly, So God you help and all saints.

[Suits in the Mayor's Court][17]

1. It is also ordained that all those who would bring suit and plead before the mayor by bill, shall find pledges and sureties to pursue their bills, and then the mayor, or the recorder, shall seal the bill with his signet, and instruct a clerk to write on the bill the date when it was

---

[16] In 1345, a French version of this oath was agreed which contained only the first four clauses and omits the fifteen days' time limit in the second clause, *CLBF*, 126; there are later French versions of the oath and a fifteenth-century English version, *CLBD*, 10, 193–4, *Liber Albus*, 313; these later versions have additional clauses preventing beadles from brewing beer for sale, keeping an oven, leasing carts or selling food.

[17] 12 Nov. 1364, the procedure outlined here was agreed, *CLBG*, 198. Sharpe does not print the regulations because John Carpenter copied them into *Liber Albus*, 390–1.

entered and accepted. And then the bill shall be delivered to a sergeant to serve the bill.

[f. 138v]

And then the mayor shall attend to the case without delay according to the use and custom of the city, or the Law Merchant.

And all the proceeds and fines that arise from such bills shall be paid to the sheriffs by their officers. And the sheriffs shall have ready every day in the mayor's court, a clerk and a sergeant to record the sheriffs' pleas that are pleaded, and to receive the fines in the following manner, that is to say:

2. For every plea of debt that amounts to 40s. or more, 12d. and no less.[18]

And if the sum be less than 40s. the fee shall be 4d. and no more.

Reserving always to the sergeants of the mayor and the Chamber, 4d. as a fee from him who recovered his debt.

But neither the sergeants, nor their yeomen, shall take anything from any defendant for their intermediary fee, except from a defendant who is acquitted because of the plaintiff's failure to pursue the case, or for any other reason, and a defendant so acquitted shall pay 4d. to the sergeants for their fee, and the plaintiff shall be fined as aforesaid the sum that he demanded in his bill for debt and damages.

3. Also saving half of the fines for affrays and bloodshed for the use of the commune, and the other half for the use of the sheriffs, as will be explained more fully later.

And if the sheriffs fail to instruct their clerks to enter such pleas, and it falls to the Chamber clerks to enter the pleas in their place, then the fines shall go to the use of the Chamber.

4. And no sergeant shall serve any bill between parties unless he has the signet seal, the pledges and the recorded date as noted above.

[f. 139]

5. And no bill is to be delayed because of defects in drafting, if there is sufficient content, the bill shall be immediately amended. The mayor shall execute due and speedy judgement to all, both strangers and denizens, who wish to enter a new plea according to the Statute of Smithfield. But if they do not begin a new plea within eight days after they made their bargain, they must abide by the common law of the city, and then they have lost the advantage of the statute.

---

[18]   In 1364 the sheriffs' officers were to receive the fee of 12d. for pleas of debt that amounted to 20s. or more, so the threshold had been raised by the time of the Jubilee Book, *Liber Albus*, 390.

[Complaints against City Officers][19]

1. Also every quarter of the year it is to be proclaimed through the city that any man who feels himself to have been wronged and wishes to complain about any extortion, wrong or grievance he has against the sheriffs' clerks, sergeants, bailiffs, beadles, constables, gaolers or other officers at Newgate, yeomen of the sergeants or other officers, he is to come to the mayor and aldermen to make his complaint.

2. The mayor, recorder and aldermen shall see that right is done in an appropriate manner, and accordingly punish the wrongdoers and chastise them as they deserve.

3. And if they fail to do right, as God defend, then he shall show his bill to the assembly chosen by the commons, and they shall pursue the matter for him to the sovereigns, so that he may have what is right and reasonable.

4. Provided always that a man who falsely complains about an officer, and who has been charged by the city in due manner, without having bribed the officer about whom he complained, then such a plaintiff shall have the same punishment that the defendant would have had if he were convicted.

The Office and Fees of the Common Sergeant at Arms[20]

1. The Common Sergeant at Arms of the city, otherwise known as the Common Crier, shall always be in the household of the mayor for the time being, and shall be ready at his command, as are the other sergeants, and shall receive 60s. every year from the Chamber and more, considering his good behaviour, if this seems reasonable to the auditors of the chamberlain's account.

And he shall receive from every alderman for his fee [f. 139v] the robes together with the cloaks in which they were sworn on the day that they took their oath of office, or else 6s. 8d. at their pleasure.

2. And he shall also take for every proclamation made in the city for the sheriffs, 12d. And so that he may do this the sheriffs should provide him with a decent horse for the honour of the city.

And also he shall have for every testament proclaimed in the Husting, and every plea determined in the Husting, 4d. for his fee.

---

[19]   Proclamations to this effect are recorded in Nov. 1378, June 1379 and Oct. 1382, *CLBH*, 112, 133, 199. The proclamations recorded in Letter-Book H do not contain clauses 3 and 4.

[20]   A French version of this passage, as far as to the end of the section on sergeants of the Chamber, has been copied into *Liber Albus*, 49–50.

N.b. And such a sergeant shall be tasked by the common council and removed when they please.

Of the Esquire and Sergeants of the Mayor

1. Also the mayor shall have at least two other sergeants, and an esquire well trained and taught, so that he can in all places perform suitable service for the honour of his lord and of the city, and to carry his sword before him, at the mayor's cost. Except that all three of them shall have 40s. each per year from the Chamber, and no more, as his allowance and salary. And the said esquire shall have, over and above this, 12d. for every letter sealed with the seal of the mayoralty, except from aldermen.

[The Sergeants of the Chamber]

1. Also there shall be three sergeants of the Chamber, and no more, to serve the chamberlain in such matters as concern the Chamber.

N.b. And they shall be chosen and removed by the common council as it pleases them. And each of them shall receive from the Chamber an annual salary of 40s.[21]

2. They shall divide between them half the 12d. fees for entering freedom bills [i.e. enrolling the names of new freemen].[22]

And they are to receive the livery of the mayor twice a year at the cost of the chamberlain.[23]

1. If any Chamber sergeant is found to be negligent, or failing to attend to his office, on the evidence of the chamberlain, at the first fault 40d. shall be deducted from his salary, and at the second, half a mark [6s. 8d.], and on the third occasion, 10s.

[f. 140]

2. It is not the intention of the common council that the sergeants shall be excused outrageous mistakes by these fines, rather, after a number of such offences, they shall be removed or punished in some other way at the discretion of the common council of the city.

---

[21] 13 Oct. 1376, William Wircestre had been elected a sergeant of the Chamber by the mayor, aldermen and commonalty, *CLBH*, 47. That the sergeants of the Chamber were to be elected by the common council would seem to be an innovation.

[22] John Carpenter noted that the fee for entering freedom bills was 40d., *Liber Albus*, 50.

[23] 19 Oct. 1377, Ralph Strode, the common pleader, had presented a petition to the mayor, aldermen and common council asking that the sergeants of the Chamber might have a common livery, like that of the sergeants of the mayor, at the city's expense. The petition was granted, *CLBH*, 81; H.T. Riley, *Memorials of London and London Life in the XIIIth, XIVth and XVth Centuries* (1868), 414–15.

[The Chamberlain, Common Sergeant at Law and Common Clerk][24]

1. Also the chamberlain,[25] common sergeant at law, otherwise known as the common narrator,[26] and the common clerk[27] are to be chosen by the common council of the said city and removed at their pleasure.

2. And each of them shall take for his labour £10 each year.

3. And above this the common clerk shall take to sustain his clerks, for every charter or deed and testament enrolled in the Husting 10*d.*, and for every deed enrolled in the rolls of the mayor 2*s.*, and for every bill of assize of nuisance and intrusion, and for every precept sent to the sheriffs for pleas in the Husting, and for every bill of *scire facias* and of *fieri facias* [procedural writs] 6*d.*, except for aldermen.

4. And the chamberlain shall present his account every year between the feasts of St. Michael [29 September] and SS. Simon and Jude [28 October] at the latest, before two aldermen and four commoners who shall be chosen by the common council of the city on St. Matthew's day [13 September] to audit the account, and they shall set a day for the chamberlain to be ready to render his account.

5. And the wardens of the bridge shall present their account every year in the same way before the same auditors, or others assigned by the common council.

[Clerks of the Chamber]

1. Also if anyone wishes to verify any record, he is to demonstrate to the chamberlain or the common clerk the reason for his request, and if this seems reasonable to the chamberlain or common clerk, he is to be shown the record by a sworn clerk of the Chamber and in no other way. And if he wishes to have a copy, he shall have it, paying a reasonable fee to the clerk who will write it.

---

[24] A French version of this section, as far as the clause relating to the mayor's clerk, is copied into *Liber Albus*, 47–9.

[25] It had been the custom for the chamberlain to be elected by the mayor, aldermen and commonalty: see the elections of Thomas de Waldene in 1349 and William Eynesham in 1374, *CLBF*, 191; *CLBG*, 326. 21 Sept. 1378, John Usshere elected chamberlain 'in a congregation of the mayor and aldermen', *CLBH*, 103. 28 May 1380, Richard Odyham elected chamberlain 'in a congregation of the mayor, aldermen and common council', *CLBH*, 149.

[26] 21 Sept. 1351, Adam de Acres, 21 Sept. 1365, John de Wentebrigge and 26 Nov. 1373, Ralph Strode, were all said to have been elected by the 'mayor, aldermen and an immense commonalty', *CLBF*, 235; *CLBG*, 199, 317. See also Barron, *London in the Later Middle Ages*, 189–90.

[27] 8 Sept. 1368, Henry de Padyngton, 9 Aug. 1375, Henry Perot, were both elected by the mayor, aldermen and commonalty, *CLBG*, 232; *CLBH*, 8; 20 Apr. 1417, John Carpenter was elected by the mayor, aldermen and common council, *CLBI*, 179.

[f. 140v]

2. And any clerk who reveals the secrets of the rolls and records in any other way and is convicted of this, he is to be bodily punished and lose his office for ever.

1. Also the chamberlain's clerk shall take in part payment for his work, half of the sums arising from the 12*d*. fee for entering freedom bills.

N.b. And over and above this he shall take for his work whatever the auditors of the chamberlain's account shall allow him, at their discretion.

1. Also the mayor at the time, who is sworn to the city and acting as escheator at that time, may take a clerk for that office [of escheator] for whom he will be answerable to the king and to the city, in salvation of his honour and his estate.

The Oath of the Chamberlain[28]

1. You shall swear that you will well and truly serve the city of London in the office of chamberlain, and whatever sums you have in your charge or keeping touching the city, you shall keep safely; and the counsels of the city you shall conceal and keep secret; you shall put right and maintain the rights of orphans as far as you can; you shall not show, or deliver, to any man, any records or muniments whereby the city might be damaged; you shall not maliciously conceal, or deny to any man, a record which he has a right to see; you shall not accept men into the franchise of the said city otherwise than is ordained in this book; you shall duly maintain the lands, tenements and rents belonging to the Chamber, and you shall increase the profits of the city as far as you reasonably can; you shall not suffer damage to the city but, as far as you can, you shall inform the mayor and the council of the city at the time about troublemakers; and in all things that pertain to your office you shall behave well and truly, as God you help and all saints.

[f. 141]

The Oath of the Common Sergeant at Law[29]

1. You shall swear that you will well and truly serve the city of London in the office of common sergeant, and the laws, customs, franchises of

---

[28] French versions of this oath are found in *CLBD*, 10 and *Liber Albus*, 309–10, and an English version in *CLBD*, 198. The only significant difference is that here the chamberlain is not to accept men into the franchise 'otherwise than is ordained in this book'.

[29] There is no earlier version of this oath. There are later versions in French in *Liber Albus*, 310 and in English in *CLBD*, 197. These versions are similar to this oath except that in the Jubilee Book the common sergeant is to attend to the needs of the city 'whenever you are required by the commons', but in the later versions this is expanded to include 'the mayor, aldermen and commons'. In the later versions he is also enjoined to secrecy.

the city you shall keep and defend within the city and without, after your skill and power; and you shall preserve and maintain the rights of orphans; you shall give good and lawful counsel in all things touching the common profit of the said city and their counsel keep; and you shall disrupt any common harm that threatens the city, or advise the council of the city about it; and whenever you are required by the commons you shall attend to the needs of the city, and where ever there shall be a need, you will show, tell and pursue it earnestly for the common profit of the city. So God you help and all saints.

The Oath of the Common Sergeant at Arms[30]

1. You shall swear that you will well and truly serve the city of London in the office of common crier, and you shall keep and defend the laws, customs and franchises of the said city, both within the city and without, to the best of your skill and power; you shall hide and conceal the counsels of the city and to the best of your ability you will disrupt any common damage which threatens the city, or you will tell the officers or council of the city about it; and you shall diligently pursue the common needs of the city at all times, as required, and in all places where there is need; and in all other matters that relate to your office, you shall conduct yourself well and truly; so God you help and all saints.

The Oath of the Common Clerk[31]

1. You shall swear that you will well and truly serve the city of London in the office of common clerk, and you shall keep and defend the laws, customs and franchises of the said city, both within the city and without, [f. 141v] to the best of your skill and power; and you shall diligently ensure that all the pleas of Husting and of Nuisance are truly entered and enrolled; and no enrolment shall be made or caused to be made by you, nor by anyone else, without the assent of the mayor and recorder; and you shall be obedient to the mayor, judges and counsel of the city, and you shall give good counsel to the best of your skill and power in all matters touching the government of the city and the common profit of the people; you shall keep secret the counsels of the city, and any common harm to the city of which you learn, you shall not allow but reveal to the officers and counsel of the city; you shall keep safely whatever money you have in your keeping belonging to the city, and you shall not show or deliver to anyone, any record or document by which the city might be damaged; you shall not maliciously conceal from anyone, or deny to him, any record to which he has a right; you shall only keep with you in court those clerks for whom you are willing to answer for at your peril and who have been sworn in the presence of

---

[30]   The only other version of this oath is in French in *Liber Albus*, 311.
[31]   The only other version of this oath is in French in *Liber Albus*, 311–12.

the mayor and aldermen; and in all other matters that pertain to your office, you shall conduct yourself well and truly, so God you help and all saints.

The Oath of the Sergeants of the Mayor and of the Chamber[32]

1. You shall swear that you will behave well and truly in your office and duly execute the charges of the mayor, aldermen and chamberlain; and you shall execute the judgements given in the mayor's court without delay; you shall not collect any fine or fees from any person, whether poor or rich, greater than those set out in the copies which are delivered to you by the court; you shall not extort money from any man by reason of your office; [f. 142] you shall report good and respectable men for inquests, and you shall not knowingly select suspect men; and you shall promote the common profit of the city as far as you can and you will not agree to act to the contrary; and you shall behave well and truly towards the common people.

2. And in all other things pertaining to your office, you shall behave well and truly, so God you help and all saints.

[The Election of the Recorder of London made by the Commons and Common Council][33]

1. It is agreed that when it is necessary to elect a recorder, a good man to occupy the office shall be chosen by a common assembly composed of the commons and the common council who shall peacefully debate, discuss and entreat among themselves who they think to be most suitable for the office, and also most profitable for the city.

2. And when they have agreed on a person, two aldermen and four commoners shall be chosen, and sent to that person, or else they will send for him, as seems best, and they will do all in their power to persuade him to take the office.

3. And if he will not take it, then another shall be chosen in the same way, and so from person to person, until someone will take the office.

4. And the recorder shall have every year for his fee, £40 from the Chamber.[34] And whenever the aldermen wear a common livery, the

---

32 This is the earliest known version of the oath. There is a later French version in *Liber Albus*, 312. In 1368 it was decided that the sergeants of the mayor, and their servants, were to be sworn to assist the mayor in keeping his oath made to the king and the city, *CLBG*, 226.

33 There is little evidence about how the recorder was chosen, but it is unlikely that he was chosen by the commons and common council acting on their own. By the fifteenth century, the recorder was chosen by the aldermen, Barron, *London in the Later Middle Ages*, 173–4.

34 This version of the recorder's remuneration predates the changes agreed at a meeting which reviewed the 'book of ordinances' held on 23 Sept. 1378. As a result of the

recorder shall wear the same livery suit of fur, at the cost of the Chamber. And the recorder shall take his meals with the mayor, if the mayor is willing, as has been customary in the past.

5. And beyond his fee he shall have 20*d.* for every charter, written testament and deed enrolled in the Husting.[35]

6. And the recorder shall not take, carry nor wear, while he is in office, any fee or robe of any foreign lord.[36] And no alderman shall be the recorder except with the assent of the common council of the city.[37]

[f. 142v]

The Oath of the Recorder[38]

1. You shall swear that you will be faithful and true to the king of England and his heirs, and to the city of London, and you shall maintain the franchises and customs of the same city, within the city and without, to the best of your power.

You shall not reveal the counsels of the city; and you shall not deviate from impartial justice for gifts, favours, promises or for hate.

You shall do right to all manner of people, poor as well as rich, denizens and strangers, who shall plead before you in the Hustings, and in all other pleas.

2. You shall truly record all the cases pleaded before you, and diligently set down and oversee that the pleas are well and truly enrolled, and no rights disturbed.

3. And you shall not delay any judgement without a reasonable cause.

And if you know of any rights or profits for the city, as in lands, tenements or rents, withheld, withdrawn, concealed or hidden, you shall reveal these to the mayor and aldermen to preserve the rights of the city.

---

complaints of William Cheyne, the recorder was awarded 40 marks (£26 13*s.* 4*d.*) from the Chamber in lieu of fees from enrolments in the husting court, in addition to his annual fee of £40, *CLBH*, 100. The recorder's annual fee in the fifteenth century was 100 marks (£66 13*s.* 4*d.*), *Liber Albus*, 43, Barron, *London in the Later Middle Ages*, 174.

35 26 Jan. 1304, *CLBC*, 153.

36 23 Sept. 1378, William Cheyne complained that his inability to receive fees or robes from foreign lords had greatly reduced his income, *CLBH*, 100.

37 29 June 1365, William de Haldane was elected as recorder and, at the same time, alderman of Tower ward, *CLBG*, 193. No subsequent recorders were also elected as aldermen, Barron, *London in the Later Middle Ages*, 173–4.

38 A French version of this oath, naming Richard [II] as king, is entered in *Liber Albus*, 308–9. An English version dating to the reign of Edward IV is recorded in *CLBD*, 33–4. The clauses relating to receiving gifts and safeguarding the 'ordinances in this book' are not found in the other versions of the oath.

4. And you shall come readily at the request of the mayor or sheriffs or their officers, to give them good and wholesome counsel to keep and maintain the good of the city.

5. And you shall be attentive to preserve and maintain the rights of orphans according to the laws and customs of the city.

And you shall not accept any gifts from any persons, great or small, if you know in your conscience that it has been sent to you to maintain some cause, or to damage or delay someone's right, rather than for love or friendship.

6. You shall not carry, wear nor take any fees or robes of any foreign lord, nor of anyone else, during your time in office.

7. You shall truly safeguard all the articles in all the ordinances in this book, and you shall not agree to any ordinances contrary to these, nor give any judgement contrary to them, without the assent of the common council of the city.

[f. 143]

You shall not behave extortionately towards any person, whether rich or poor, by colour of your office.

8. And in all other things pertaining to your office you shall behave well and truly, so God help you and all saints.

The Election of Aldermen[39]

1. Also in the right election of aldermen each one shall be chosen by the ward where he shall be alderman, and his name presented to the mayor by the greater part of the good men, with the officers of the same ward, and there he will be received and take his charge.

2. And every ward that lacks an alderman because of death, or because the alderman was removed for any other true cause, then they should choose another within fifteen days from being warned by the mayor of the vacancy. And if the ward has not agreed on an election within the said fifteen days, then, in default, the mayor with the advice of the

---

[39] 8 June 1319, Letters patent of Edward II laid down that new aldermen were to be elected annually on the feast of St. Gregory the Pope (12 Mar.). This injunction was largely ignored until further royal Letters Patent dated 2 Nov. 1376 re-iterated that new aldermen should be elected annually. These letters patent have been copied into this book, see pp. 122–3. 6 Mar. 1377, common council confirmed the practice of annual elections, *CLBH*, 60. 29 Jan. 1384, it was decided that aldermen might be re-elected, *CLBH*, 227. In the Parliament that sat from Jan. to Mar. 1394, it was decided that aldermen should, again, serve for life, unless removed for reasonable causes *CLBH*, 409–10; *PROME*, vii. 266. See *Liber Albus*, 36, 39–40; Barron, *London in the Later Middle Ages*, 137–8.

aldermen, shall appoint a suitable man to govern the said ward for the remaining time.[40]

3. And if the man chosen by the ward, or by the mayor, refuses the office, he shall lose his freedom and he shall not be restored to the freedom except by payment of a fine agreed by the common council of the city.

The Oath of the Alderman[41]

1. You shall swear that you will well and truly serve the king and the city of London in the office of alderman in the ward for which you have been chosen alderman.

And you shall truly advise and inform the people in your ward about the things they must do to guard and keep the city, and to maintain peace in the ward.

And you shall keep and maintain the laws and customs and freedoms of the said city, both within the city and without, to the best of your ability and power.

And you shall be attentive to the rights of orphans, to preserve and maintain them in accordance with the laws and customs of the city.

[f. 143v]

2. And you shall be ready to come speedily when summoned and warned by the mayor and officers of the city of the time, for the sessions, pleas and judgements in the Hustings, and to be employed on other needs of the city, if you are not prevented by the needs of our lord the king, or by other reasonable cause.

And you shall give good, lawful and true counsel about matters touching the common profit of the city.

And you shall take no gift from any person, great or small, if you believe in your conscience, that it has been sent to you to maintain some cause, or to damage or delay someone's right, rather than for love or friendship.

---

[40] 22 May 1375, William Walworth, mayor, agreed to transfer William Haldane from Cheap to Lime Street ward, and Adam Stable was moved from Coleman Street to Cheap, without any reference to the men of the wards concerned, *CLBH*, 7. This may have provoked these regulations.

[41] An earlier French version of this oath is found in *CLBD*, 12, 13 and later versions in French, *Liber Albus*, 307–8 and in English, *CLBD*, 205. The four final clauses of the oath as recorded here are not found in the other versions. 7 Jan. 1383, a clause added to the alderman's oath to maintain regulations about the sale of fish in the city made in the Parliament of Nov. 1382, *PROME*, vi. 301–4. The relevant part of the statute has been copied into the Jubilee Book, see below pp. 123–4. This statute was repealed the following year in Parliament Nov. 1383, *PROME*, vi. 345–6; *Calendar of Charter Rolls 1341–1417*, p. 294.

And you shall truly maintain all the ordinances in this book, in all their articles, and you shall not agree to any ordinances or judgements contrary to these, without the agreement of the common council of the city.

3. And you shall ensure the due execution of presentments in your wardmote and purposefully pursue them.

You shall not behave extortionately towards any person, whether poor or rich, by colour of your office. You shall well and truly conduct yourself in the said office, and in all other matters in which you are involved touching the city, so God you help and all saints.

[Duties of Aldermen]

1. Whenever the aldermen agree on a common livery, the clothing shall not be given away, nor otherwise transferred within two years, upon payment of a fine of 100s. to the Chamber.

2. And if any alderman dies within the [two-year] term, his executors shall keep the same clothing without disposing of it until the two years is up, upon the same penalty.[42]

3. Also no alderman in future may exchange wards with another alderman, nor move from ward to ward, without the assent of the common council of the city.

[f. 144]

1. And that no-one who is or who has been alderman or sheriff is to be put on a jury.

2. In future there shall be no seizure, yielded up or covered up, of lands or tenements except in the presence of the beadle or other good men of the neighbourhood. And he that takes the seizure shall pay 2s. to the alderman and 6d. to the beadle.

3. And if the seizure is done secretly, in the absence of the beadle and neighbours, then he shall pay a double fee to the alderman and to the beadle, and also 20s. to the Chamber.

But seizure of a quitrent, or a rent charge, or grant of reversion, may be carried out by an enrolled deed without the presence of the beadle or others, as has been customary in the past.

---

[42]   8 Jan. 1358, these regulations about the livery of aldermen agreed, *CLBG*, 93; also copied into *Liber Albus*, 35.

[The Wardmote][43]

1. Every alderman shall hold his wardmote four times a year if necessary, and at least twice, when he shall diligently examine the points written below, and he shall deal as speedily as possible with all nuisances presented to him, on pain of a fine of 40s. payable to the Chamber if he is considered to have been negligent.

All those who have houses or smaller chambers within the same ward shall attend the wardmote together with all servants over the age of fifteen, except apprentices.

And all those who have not already been sworn in the ward, shall be put into frankpledge [A system whereby men became mutually responsible for their good behaviour], even if they have previously been sworn in another ward where they lived before.

And everyone received into frankpledge shall pay 1d. for his entrance fee.

2. And anyone who is absent without reasonable excuse shall pay 4d. to the alderman, unless he be a clerk, knight or woman.

3. And the alderman should himself investigate nuisances in his ward on a daily basis without delay, in order to make due correction, unless [f. 144v] the matter is particularly difficult and hard and should be brought to the attention of the mayor.[44]

4. And if he finds the officers of the ward to be negligent in carrying out their office, he should instruct them to improve, and if they are disobedient he should punish them, or report them to the mayor, and pursue the matter until they are punished as they deserve.

The Oath of those entering Frankpledge[45]

1. You shall swear that you will be true and faithful to the king of England and to his heirs, and you shall keep the king's peace, and obey the officers of the city, and arrest wrongdoers and those who break the king's peace.

And you shall be ready at all times to help the said officers when warned by the constables and beadles to join the watch or other tasks to safeguard the peace, both denizens and strangers.

---

43   John Carpenter describes the procedure for summoning a wardmote meeting and includes some of the regulations listed here but does not include the 40s. fine imposed on an alderman for negligence, *Liber Albus*, 37–8.

44   John Carpenter's version of this clause omits the requirement to examine nuisances on a daily basis and allows that some of the problems may relate to the city Chamber, *Liber Albus*, 39.

45   There are later French versions of this oath, *CLBD*, 10; *Liber Albus*, 315.

And well and truly to observe and maintain the articles of this wardmote.

2. And if you know of any evil gathering or fellowship within the ward, or the city, you shall inform the alderman about it.

And in all other ways you shall behave and speak as good and true men behave, so God you help and all saints.

How the wardmote shall be held

1. Every baker, when he is warned to do so by the beadle, should bring his mark once a year to the wardmote, and there his name shall be entered together with the figure of his mark, and he shall pay 4*d*. the first time his name and mark are entered.[46]

And at the wardmote the constables, scavengers and beadles shall be chosen and removed by the good men of the ward in which they are officers as seems necessary.[47]

[f. 145]

And no one shall be chosen for office unless he is a freeman of the city, and a true man and of good reputation.

And if anyone who is chosen as a constable or scavenger refuse the office, he shall pay a fine of 20*s*. to the Chamber without remission.

And the alderman should instruct his clerk to read aloud in English the following points: the places where the beadle will summon as many good people as necessary to the inquest, who shall be charged to enquire honestly, and the scavengers and beadles shall join them on the inquest to provide information.

Every beadle may levy within his bailiwick for debt to the amount of 5*s*. But the man who has been levied may, if he wishes, challenge the levy in the sheriffs' court to be restored, and have the case settled there.

These points are to be read out in the full wardmote which all the people of the ward shall be charged to obey faithfully

[Articles of the Wardmote][48]

First it shall be enquired if the peace of our lord the king is anything but well kept, and if not who is at fault and by whom has it been broken or disturbed.

---

46 See *Liber Albus*, 38.

47 *Ibid.*

48 Articles of the wardmote were compiled at different times and reflect current concerns. An earlier list of articles was drawn up in Dec. 1370 regulating the prices of food, especially wine, poultry and corn, *CLBG*, 271–2. Two later lists found in *Liber Albus*, 257–60, 332–8, are largely the same as the lists here. Those articles that do not appear later in *Liber Albus* are marked *.

And if there are any persons temporarily resident or frequenting the ward that are not in frankpledge, and if there are any coming to the ward who are outlaws or convicted felons;

Also whether any person makes scot ale [i.e. holds a drinking party] or is a receiver or convener of evil company, and if any be common rioters or tricksters or nightwalkers without lights, contrary to the mayor's proclamation;

Also if any innkeeper, taverner or brewer keeps his premises open after the hour set by the mayor;[49]

*Also if there are any pimps, habitual gamblers, troublemakers, maintainers of quarrels, maintainers of false legal suits for profit, bribers of juries, or other wrongdoers living in the ward;

Also if any bawd, common prostitute, witch, scold or huckster of ale lives within the ward;

[f. 145v]

Also if there are any who will not help the constables and officers to keep the peace and arrest wrongdoers at the calling of the hue and cry;

*Also if any parish clerk rings the curfew after the curfew has been rung at Bow church, Barking church, St. Bride's and St. Giles Cripplegate;[50]

Also if any officer is extortionate by virtue of his office, or maintains quarrels contrary to right, or takes carts or arrests victuals unreasonably;

*Also if anyone has acted contrary to the mayor's proclamation in any points.

Articles touching the control of victuals and victuallers

*Whether anyone who forestalls victuals or other merchandise coming to the city to be sold, is living in the ward;

*Whether any victualler sells food that is unsuitable or noxious for human consumption, or whether they are selling it a price higher than that ordained by the mayor;

Whether anyone is selling wine or ale above the ordained price, and other than in sealed measures, and whether anyone sells ale to a huckster to sell on;

---

49   5 June 1378, proclamation, *CLBH*, 93.
50   May 1378, proclamation, *CPMR 1364–1381*, p. 219 and. 22 Apr. 1469, *CLBL*, 84. The churches were St. Mary le Bow, in Cheapside, All Hallows Barking, near the Tower, St. Bride's in Fleet Street, to the west of the city and St. Giles, Cripplegate, to the north. John Carpenter names only three curfew churches: St. Martin le Grand, All Hallows Barking and St. Lawrence (probably St. Lawrence Jewry near Guildhall rather than St. Lawrence Pountney near the Thames), *Liber Albus*, 275.

Whether anyone is buying or selling using unsealed measures or weights, or using one measure for buying, and another for selling;

Whether any innkeeper is baking bread within his inn, and whether any baker bakes white or brown bread to sell without a mark, or charges more than 1d. for baking a bushel.

Articles touching encroachments and other defaults

*Whether anyone is concealing the goods of orphans which are the concern of the Chamber of the Guildhall;

Whether anyone in the ward has encroached onto the common soil, whether with walls, fences, stalls, bollards or cellar doors;

Whether any overhanging jetty is so low as to obstruct riders or carriages;

[f. 146]

Whether anyone throws dung, ordure, rubbish, carcasses or other offensive things in front of their neighbour's door, or casts water or other liquids out of their doors or windows by day or night;

Whether any common way, or common watercourse, is blocked or stopped or impeded to the nuisance of the ward, and who is doing this;

*Whether any pavement is defective, either too high or too low, to trouble riders or carriages;

Whether anyone keeps swine, cattle, oxen, cows or calves or ducks to the annoyance of their neighbours.

Articles against the perils of fire

Whether any house is roofed other than with tiles, stone or lead, for fear of fire;

Whether any chimney, hearth or furnace is dangerous or not in compliance with civic ordinances made to avoid the perils of fire;

*Whether any brewer brews, or baker bakes, using straw or other fire-hazard fuels;

Whether any leper, cheater or shameless beggar is loitering in the ward.

Articles for officers and other matters necessary for the ward

*The good men of the ward should find and choose ward officers, that is, constables, scavengers, ale-conners, a beadle and a raker, who should be sworn before the alderman to perform their office well and truly.

They should also acquire a strong iron hook with a chain, and ropes, and two long ladders to use in case of fire.[51]

---

[51] 25 July 1376, mayoral precept, *CLBH*, 28.

Also every house should keep a tub full of water before the door in summer time, to use in case of fire.[52]

[f. 146v]

*Also if any common wrongdoers, or suspected persons, are presented to the alderman by the good men of the ward, then they shall immediately be arrested by the alderman and sheriffs, or by their officers if they are not present. But if they are present, then it shall be done at the alderman's command, and they, and their goods, shall be kept securely until they can be brought before the mayor and aldermen. And there they shall be told why they have been arrested and presented, and those that cannot acquit themselves shall be punished by imprisonment or other punishment at the discretion of the mayor and aldermen, provided that the offence was not violent. But if the offence was violent, then the common council shall advise on the punishment.

Of the Election of Sheriffs[53]

The right to elect the sheriffs belongs to the mayor, recorder, aldermen and commons assembled on St. Matthew's day [21 September] in the same way as that laid down for the election of the mayor.[54]

And the mayor shall first of his free will choose a good man free of the city as one of the sheriffs for the following year and he [the mayor] will answer for half the city's farm [the fixed sum annually payable to the king by the city] owed to the king if the man he has chosen is not sufficiently wealthy. But if the mayor has chosen the sheriff by the advice, and with the assent, of the aldermen, then they ought to answer [for half of the farm] with the mayor.

And the other sheriff shall be chosen by the commons, and by those summoned by the mayor for that purpose as is before laid down; and [in this case] the commons should answer for the other half of the farm owed to the king, if the man chosen is not sufficiently wealthy.

And if any controversy arises between the commons over the election then it shall be dealt with as laid down in the ordinance dealing with the election of the mayor.

---

52 25 July 1376, mayoral precept, 5 June 1378, proclamation, *CLBH*, 28, 92.
53 John Carpenter's chapter on '*Vicecomitum Electio*' is exactly the same as this section of the Jubilee Book, *Liber Albus*, 43–5.
54 See above p. 87. 20 June 1384, decided by the mayor, aldermen and 'good and sufficient men summoned from the wards' that for the election of the sheriffs, the mayor should summon the common council and others of the more sufficient men of the city, to elect an able person who would be presented to the mayor and aldermen by their common sergeant, *CLBH*, 241.

[f. 147]

And if any of those chosen to be sheriff shall refuse, or stays away so that he is not ready at the Guildhall on the eve of St. Michael's day [28 September] following, at ten o'clock, to take his charge, then £100 shall be immediately levied from the goods, lands and tenements of the man who is absent, one half to go to the Chamber and the other half to the man who is then suddenly chosen and charged as a result of his absence.[55]

And if the second man who is chosen shall refuse the charge, then all his goods, lands and tenements shall be taken by the city, and the man who takes the charge in his place shall have all the arrested goods, lands and tenements to use to defray all the costs of that office.

And the old sheriffs shall come to the Guildhall at eleven o'clock at the latest and deliver the cocket [seal] to the mayor in full court. And they shall also at the latest deliver to the mayor at his general court held at the next feast of Epiphany [6 January] all the records of the pleas touching free tenements pleaded before them during their term of office, together with all the records touching the recoveries [fines] of any person, on pain of a fine of 100s. to be paid by each of them for the use of the Chamber. And the mayor is to remind them about this on the day that they take up office.

Then the mayor shall deliver the cocket to the sheriff whom he has chosen, and the records to the chamberlain for safe-keeping, and then the new sheriffs shall be charged as follows:

The Oath of the Sheriffs[56]

You shall swear to be faithful and true to our lord the king and to his heirs, and you shall preserve and maintain the franchises of the city of London, within and without the city, to the best of your power and be obedient to the mayor at the time, *and send those arrested by the mayor and aldermen to one of your counters to keep securely, [f. 147v] *and not release anyone on security [bail] without the assent of the mayor and aldermen.

You shall obey the mayor's reasonable commands and you shall well and truly keep the counties and shires of London and Middlesex.

---

55 21 Sept. 1350, decided by mayor, aldermen and 'whole commonalty' that a man who refused to take up the office of sheriff was to be fined £100, *CLBF*, 306.

56 There is an earlier French version of this oath and a later one in *CLBD*, 11; *Liber Albus*, 306. There is an English version *temp.* Henry VI, *CLBD*, 206–07. None of these versions of the oath contains the clauses marked *. 7 Jan. 1383, an additional clause added to the sheriff's oath to maintain the ordinances relating to the sale of fish made in the last Parliament, see n. 41 above.

You shall well and truly carry out the tasks relating to those shires to the best of your power.

You shall do right to poor as to rich without any extortion to any by reason of your office.

You shall not damage good customs nor encourage evil ones.

You shall well and truly observe, and cause to be observed, the assizes of bread and ale and other assizes which are your responsibility both within the franchises of the city and without.

You shall not delay judgements and the business of your courts except for good reasons, and you shall not impede the rights of others.

You shall not return writs sent to you touching the estate and franchise of the city before you have shown them to the mayor and aldermen at the time, and to the [legal] counsel of the city if need be, and that you take heed of their advice.

You shall be ready, if given reasonable warning by the mayor, to keep and maintain the peaceable state of the city.

*You shall not accept any gift from anyone, lesser or greater, unless you are sure in your conscience that it is not given to you to maintain a quarrel, or deflect the course of justice, but from true love and friendship.

*You shall maintain all the ordinances in this book, in all their articles, and you shall not assent to any ordinances or judgements contrary to this, unless with the assent of the common council of the city.

You shall not farm [lease out] the shire of Middlesex, nor the gaol of Newgate, and all that relates to your office and to the keeping of the said shires, you and your servants shall faithfully execute.

[f. 148]

You shall preserve the said city from damage as far as you are able.

*Half the fines for affrays of bloodshed occurring during your time, you shall faithfully deliver, or see that they are delivered, to the chamberlain.

*You shall have no more than four sergeants.[57]

You shall behave well and truly in your office, and in all matters in which you are involved touching the said city, so God you help and all saints.

---

[57]   28 Sept. 1356, sheriffs to have two sergeants 'and more if necessary', *CLBG*, 72; 21 Sept. 1375, Ralph Strode petitioned on behalf of the commonalty that the sheriffs should have no more than three or four sergeants 'in order that the people might no longer suffer from an excessive number', *CLBH*, 12; 21 Sept. 1378, seven sheriffs' sergeants sworn, *CLBH*, 102; 9 Nov. 1403, no sheriff to have more than eight sergeants, *CLBI*, 32. See *Liber Albus*, 527; Barron, *London in the Later Middle Ages*, 170–1.

And immediately after the sheriffs are sworn, all their officers, that is, clerks, sergeants and their yeomen, bailiffs of customs and of Middlesex, the gaoler of Newgate and his clerk, shall be sworn, each according to his office, notwithstanding that they may already have sworn an oath to their masters.

And anyone who refuses to take an oath shall be deprived of all offices for that year.

And anyone who fails to appear before the mayor and aldermen to take his oath shall lose all offices for that year.

No sheriff shall have more than four sergeants unless it is necessary to carry out tasks for the people's needs.[58]

The Oath of the Undersheriff and of all the Clerks of the Sheriffs[59]

[1.] You shall swear that you will well and truly serve your masters, the sheriffs of London and Middlesex, chosen for the coming year,

and you will not be swayed by gift, nor favour, nor promise, nor hate, and that you will do right by all people, poor and rich, denizens and strangers, who shall plead before you without any bias in any quarrel.

[2.] You shall, as far as you can, only summon good, true and law-abiding men to serve on inquests and juries, and not those who are partisan, or paid by parties [to the dispute].

[f. 148v]

[3.] You shall record accurately all the pleas heard before you, and you shall work diligently to ensure and check that the said pleas have been well and truly entered and enrolled.

[4.] You shall not obstruct anyone's rights, nor act extortionately on account of your office, or the office of your masters.

[5.] You shall not delay any judgement without good reason.

[6.] You shall keep and maintain the franchise of the city to the best of your power.

---

58 See n. 57.
59 The scribe has here conflated the earlier oaths of the undersheriff and the sheriffs' clerks, both written in French, *CLBD*, 3, 12–13. The same conflated oath is found in French in *Liber Albus*, 317–18. In the earlier oaths, clause 11 is omitted, and the aldermen are omitted from clauses 10 and 13, also the advice given to the mayor and judges is to be kept secret (clause 7) and the emphasis on secrecy is again reiterated in the version in *Liber Albus*. There is a much shorter oath for the sheriffs' clerks recorded c. 1345, *CLBF*, 125–6. In 1368 it was decided that the sheriffs' clerks were to be sworn to the mayor and the city in the Guildhall 'as aforetime', *CLBG*, 226.

[7.] You shall obey the mayor and judges of the city, and you shall, when required, give them good advice for the common profit of the people.

[8.] You shall not bribe, or embezzle, or fine anyone at a higher rate than is laid down by the common council of the city and you shall account honestly to the chamberlain, as has been ordained, for fines arising from affrays and blood-shedding, without concealing anything.

[9.] You shall not allow your deputies to impose any charges that are not owed and reasonable and customary in the city.

[10.] You shall not return writs that come to you touching the estate and franchise of the city without first showing them to the mayor and aldermen at the time, and taking their advice.

[11.] You shall truly levy the proceeds, fines and penalties that come to you under green wax or the pipe, without any increase, and those who have paid you shall honestly discharge and not make further demands on them.

[12.] You shall charge the sergeants' yeomen who take the fees for carriage in the city, that they shall not charge more for carriage than they ought to take, and that they do not charge carriage fees for those bringing victuals into the city.

[13.] You shall not give any judgement contrary to any ordinance made by the mayor, aldermen and common council of the city, unless it has been cut or amended by them.

[f. 149]

[14.] You shall act well and truly in these and all other things relating to your office, so God you help and all saints.

The Oath of the Sheriffs' Sergeants[60]

You shall swear that you will behave well and truly in your office, and be obedient to the mayor and judges of the city, and you shall save and maintain their honour as far as you can.

You shall not levy fines or penalties, whether from poor or rich, greater than those contained in the instructions delivered to you by the courts.

You shall not behave extortionately by colour of your office, and you shall truly and without delay, carry out in due and diligent manner whatsoever you shall be charged to do by the rulers of the city.

You shall return good men and true for inquests, and not men known to you as suspicious or bribed.

---

[60]   This oath varies considerably from the earlier French version in *CLBD*, ii, but is almost exactly the same as the version in *Liber Albus*, 318–19.

You shall not delay matters for your own profit and you shall to the best of your ability and power uphold the ordinances which the common council has agreed, to maintain the king's peace and the common profit.

You shall conduct and behave yourself well and peaceably towards the common people.

So God you help and all saints.

The Oath of the Sergeants' Yeomen[61]

You shall swear that you will be obedient to the mayor and rulers of the city, and that you will not, by colour of your office, behave extortionately.

You shall take no more than is necessary, nor oppress, from the goods of those bringing food to the city by way of carriage.

You shall carry out all the punishments following judgements with which you are charged by your rulers, in a good manner [f. 149v] and correctly, without complaint, both in private and openly.

And in all other matters you shall act and speak as good and true men behave. So God you help and all saints.

[The Duties of the Sheriffs][62]

Also the same day, after dinner, the old and new sheriffs shall go together to the prison at Newgate, and there the new sheriffs shall take charge of all the prisons and prisoners by an indenture made between them and the old sheriffs. They are to keep the prisons securely, at their peril; and they are not to let the gaol to farm [lease it out].

And it is to be known that all the profits from any customs or bailiwicks belonging to the sheriffs of London and Middlesex arising after noon on the eve of St. Michael [28 September] abovesaid shall belong to the new sheriffs, and those arising before noon, to the old sheriffs.

No sheriff in future is to fine any baker or brewer more highly than at the ordained rate. And if any sheriff does this, and is convicted, he shall be required to pay for every penny so taken, or received, 12*d.* to the Chamber.

N.b. And if it should happen, which God forfend, that any sheriff, or their officers, having received a specific command from the mayor or aldermen to carry out some task in the city, and the sheriff, or his

---

61 There is no earlier version of this oath recorded. The later French oath is the same as this version although the entry is headed '*Sacramentum Garconum Vicecomitum*', *Liber Albus*, 319.

62 A French version of this passage as far as 'without restitution' is found in *Liber Albus*, 45–6.

officers, refuse to do it; then the sheriff or his officer shall immediately be warned to appear before the mayor and aldermen and common council of the city to explain why he has not done as he was ordered. And if he fails to come on the appointed day, or if he comes but provides no reasonable answer or excuse, then he shall lose his office and someone else will be appointed in his place.

And if a fault is found in a sheriff's officer, then he shall lose his office and be forever excluded from holding office in the city in the future, without restitution.

[f. 150]

And that no [clerks of the] mayor, sheriffs or aldermen, nor clerks of the sheriffs, nor of the Chamber sergeant nor any beadle, nor sergeants' yeomen, nor porters at the counters, nor the officers at Newgate, nor their valets, yeomen or sergeants, are in future to undertake brewing on their own or anyone else's account to sell, nor keep a bakery, nor hire carts, nor act as regraters [who buy up goods for resale before they come to market] of victuals, nor as hucksters [sellers] of ale, nor as their partners. And those that will not swear to observe this, or act contrary to this ordinance, shall lose their office forever.[63]

The sheriffs, or their clerks on their behalf, shall twice a year, namely at Easter and Michaelmas [29 September], render true account with the chamberlain, without any concealment or hiding of the fines paid for affrays and bloodshed, and they shall deliver whole to the chamberlain half the money arising from these fines without withholding anything. And they are to keep the other half of the fines for their trouble.

[Procedure in the Sheriffs' Courts][64]

Also the sheriffs shall deal with the pleas of debt, trespass, covenant, detinue [suit for the recovery of goods wrongfully withheld] and account, pending or hanging before them, whether between foreigner and foreigner, or between foreigner and denizen, from one day to the next without delay, after dinner at their counters,[65] as well as before at Guildhall. And if the case is not pleaded, it shall be determined by inquest, so that if

---

63 7 Jan. 1383, this regulation agreed in common council, *CLBH*, 209–10.

64 The procedures in the sheriffs' courts were clearly of concern since seven folios are devoted to them. 28 Sept. 1356, these procedures had been reviewed and reformed by the mayor, aldermen and 'an immense commonalty', *CLBG*, 71–5. Some of these regulations are incorporated in the Jubilee Book, but there are many differences. The account to be found in *Liber Albus* is also very different from the Jubilee Book, *Liber Albus*, 199–223. The procedures in the sheriffs' courts and the conduct of their officers were further regulated in 1393 and these later regulations were (with a few exceptions) copied into *Liber Albus*, see LBH, ff. 286–286v and *Liber Albus*, 519–25.

65 The two sheriffs' counters (or compters) were usually located in, or near, Bread Street and Poultry.

a foreigner is not continually residing or abiding within the franchise of the city, then those that are residing in the city, may have their plea proceedings as if they were frank and free denizens [i.e. as freemen]. And if such a foreigner, remaining or continuously living within the franchise, wages his law [swears to the truth of his case by the use of oath helpers], he shall make his law by six hands as free denizens do.

[f. 150v]

And let it be known that every foreign defendant who does not stay or live in the city, who is allowed to make his law by his own hand alone, shall be sworn in court. And furthermore he shall make the same oath in six parish churches, according to ancient custom, if the plaintiff demands it.

And no writ of *capias* [for seizing a person] shall be awarded against a defendant denizen unless the sergeant testifies that he has nothing within the franchise which may be seized, as the plaintiff shall swear, or if two good neighbours testify that the defendant is fugitive [i.e. has fled the city's jurisdiction]. But a writ of *capias* may always be awarded against a foreign defendant right away if the plaintiff will not at his peril certify to the court that the defendant has goods in the hands of a third party, [or is owed goods by a third party]. And if the sheriff, undersheriff or his clerk, will not award the writ of *capias* right away, or a writ of attachment [for seizing his goods] on such a foreigner or his goods, at the request of a man who is frank and free of the city, then the sheriff shall settle with the plaintiff the damages that he incurred through the failure to award a writ of *capias*, or writ of attachment in the case where the defendant is outside the franchise, in accordance with the advice of the mayor, aldermen and common council.

Also, if any freeman of the city wages his law in a court of record, as if he were a foreigner, so as to escape [by swearing] with his hand, sole or alone, he shall lose his freedom and will never be restored without paying a fine, which the chamberlain shall be instructed to collect, on the advice of the mayor and common council.

If any married woman covered by her husband practices a craft by herself, whereby she buys and sells victuals, or other merchandise that relates to her craft, and she and her husband are prosecuted for something that she has bought and bargained for, [f. 151] and the husband does not appear in court to answer in the case, then the wife may take up the issue and receive judgement as if she were single. And in cases where the plaintiff shall sue by foreign writ of attachment, he shall execute all the husband's goods found within the city franchise.[66]

---

[66] Carpenter also describes the rights of a married woman who trades apart from her husband, but he incorporates greater protection for the goods of the husband, *Liber Albus*, 204–5.

Also, if anyone offers to wage his law, and then fails to do so, judgement shall be given right away, without awaiting the presence of the plaintiff and then execution shall be carried out on him [the defaulting plaintiff] and his guarantors. And if the plaintiff defaults then he shall immediately be subject to a judgement blocking prosecution of his suit and lose his plea.

If any defendant in a plea of debt, trespass of account, detinue or covenant made within the franchise of London, produces an acquittance [release] made in the countryside where the contract was not made, or where the court may have no cognisance or knowledge, the acquittance will be discounted. But they are to proceed to judgement notwithstanding if the defendant is unable to answer the charge, and the plaintiff swears upon examination in the Mayor's Court that the acquittance was not of his making.

Also an executor shall answer for his testator for things done within the franchise as follows: that is to wit that the executor shall swear, together with as many persons as the court shall think reasonable, that he had not heard, seen, found nor had any knowledge that the testator was liable for the demand.[67]

No panel of jurors shall, in future, be arranged to be impanelled between two parties within the franchise [f. 151v] before justices, the mayor or the sheriffs, on any chargeable matter except in the presence, and by the advice, of the mayor, recorder and two aldermen chosen by the mayor and without the incitement of the parties, and also at least one of the sheriffs if any of the parties wishes it.

And that panel of jurors empanelled by them should be summoned, and no other. And the same procedure should be followed from now onwards in the case of the twelve, eight or six accusations, whether they be at St. Martin le Grand before the justices of *nisi prius*,[68] or at other inquests in the city of London before the mayor or sheriffs, as well as for the king [cases to which the Crown was party] as between party and party, they are to be composed of good people, true and qualified and not of doubtful character.

Also the mayor and recorder shall supervise, and change if necessary, the panels of jurors empanelled in the Husting by the beadle, if either of the parties demands it, as is the case with other inquests.

---

67 The responsibilities of executors for the debts of testators were clearly a cause for concern, see decision of common council, 12 Mar. 1379, *CLBH*, 122.

68 A writ of *nisi prius* referred a suit from one of the King's courts to the justices of assize who in London sat at St. Martin le Grand.

And if those summoned do not turn up in court to answer to their names, on the first day they shall be fined, and on the second day a double fine, and on the third day all their goods shall be seized.

Also in no court in the city before the mayor or sheriffs, shall any judgement be delayed beyond the third court after judgement was due to be given, unless the matter is generally agreed to be especially difficult and so needing longer time for deliberation.

Also all men who bring a case for recovery of debt, after their recovery, shall have their damages awarded to them by the court or by the inquest. The debtor shall be imprisoned until satisfaction is made to the plaintiff, both for the damages awarded to him, as well as for the principal debt.

But if the plaintiff produces an obligation [sealed bond] made to him by the defendant, and the defendant falsely denies it, and is convicted of that; then the damages shall be awarded in accordance with the length of time the payment has been overdue, by order of the court.

[f. 152]

And he shall be imprisoned according to the Common Law.

Also no plaintiff shall be forced to pay anything for the entry of his personal plea, and the plaintiff shall be ready in court with his attorney for him to pursue his complaint, without being allowed to excuse his absence on pain of a judgement blocking prosecution of his suit.

And the plea shall always be entered on the roll on the day when the plea was made, otherwise it will be held for naught, so that it may be known who was the first plaintiff in a case, where many foreign attachments are made.

And if it happens that one roll contains many pleas against one person, the plea that is written first in the roll, shall be considered the first. But it is to be noted that the man at whose suit the defendant was first arrested, shall have his plea dealt with first, even if someone else had brought his case earlier, unless someone was arrested at the suit of one plaintiff, and then another plaintiff claims certain of the defendant's goods within the franchise. In this case the second plaintiff shall have first execution of the goods of the defendant, if those goods are sufficient to satisfy both plaintiffs. But if the goods are only sufficient to satisfy the second plaintiff at whose suit they were arrested, then he shall have the execution of them, and the first plaintiff shall have the defendant arrested bodily at his suit. And all cases where there are many attachments upon various goods of a single defendant at the suit of many plaintiffs, shall be dealt with in the same way.

And the sheriffs' clerks shall enter in the rolls all the cases pleaded before them if the plaintiff demands it.

And the sheriff should ensure that he has the defendant bodily arrested until the case is fully settled and finished, [f. 152v] on pain of answering to the plaintiff for such sum as it seems likely he would have recovered from the defendant if he had been present.

Also, if anyone brings a plea against another, and his case is tried by due process and found to be false, then damages are to be judged to the defending party at the discretion of the court, taking into account the trouble, expense and costs that the defendant has incurred and suffered in that case.

Also, if it happens in any court when men are suing each other, that the defending party claims that the plea is untrue and demands that the plaintiff swear an oath with his own hand alone and the plaintiff will not swear that his action is true, then the defendant is judged to be acquitted, and the plaintiff shall be fined. And the same law applies if the defendant refuses to swear when challenged to do so by the plaintiff.[69]

Also if after the giving of a judgement, but before its execution, the defendant buys a writ of error to bring the record of the case before the mayor or justices whereby the execution of the judgement, and the recovery by the plaintiff, is delayed; in such a case the goods of the first defendant arrested, found within the franchise, shall be seized and arrested to the value of what was judged, together with the damages and penalties, and kept safely and securely during the plea of error, so that the execution of the first judgement may be carried out in due manner, provided that the first judgement is upheld by the mayor or justices, and provided that the first defendant is not in prison because of the first judgement.

[f. 153]

But it shall be lawful for the first defendant, if he chooses, to provide surety for the aforesaid goods.

And no man, who is free of the city, is to sue for a writ of record and process from the city before the justices at St. Martin le Grand before he has shown his grievances to the mayor and aldermen to examine the matters and to redress what is amiss if they can and will do so, without long delay, upon pain of losing the freedom for ever and paying a fine of £10 to the city. But if the mayor and aldermen cannot, or will not, correct the errors without a long delay, then he may take his case afresh to the justices at St. Martin le Grand without being stopped.

---

[69]   28 Sept. 1356, this regulation agreed by the mayor, aldermen, sheriffs and 'an immense commonalty'. *CLBG*, 73. The *quid pro quo* for the plaintiff is not included in the earlier regulation, but is included in the detailed regulations relating to the sheriffs' courts drawn up in 1393 which were then copied into *Liber Albus*, see LBH, f. 286v, and *Liber Albus*, 521.

And no freeman may sue another freeman in a plea outside the city which could be duly determined before the judges of the city, unless he has a licence from the mayor and aldermen for a good reason, upon pain of losing his freedom, which he may not regain except by paying a fine to the Chamber, to be determined by the mayor, aldermen and common council of the city.

Also the sheriffs of the city shall hold the assizes of *novel disseisin* [to deal with complaints relating to recent unlawful dispossession] every week and the assizes of *mort d'ancestor* [to deal with the complaints of dispossessed heirs] every fortnight.[70]

And the sheriffs and coroner are not to be absent in order to cause the parties wilful delaying of the law, upon pain of at least 100s. each to the Chamber.

The sheriffs should not farm [lease out] the county of Middlesex in any way unless it is properly controlled by their deputy so that the people of the said county and shire of Middlesex may be treated and governed in due manner as required by law, and with no extortion.[71]

[f. 153v]

Also the sheriffs may not farm [lease out] the gaol of Newgate, but they shall appoint a qualified man of good reputation to keep the gaol appropriately without charging him for the keepership either by an open, or secret, agreement.[72]

And the gaoler appointed by the said sheriffs shall swear before the mayor and aldermen that neither he, nor anyone acting on his behalf, shall take money, or extort money, from any prisoner for placing or removing him from his irons and fetters, or extort anything from prisoners. But it shall be lawful for the gaoler to take 4d. from every prisoner delivered out of prison as is customary except that he may not take anything suddenly from any man at his entry or exit by command of the mayor and aldermen, without other process. And if it is found that he has behaved extortionately to anyone, he is to lose his office and be punished at the discretion of the mayor, aldermen and common council of the city.

Also every yeoman of the sergeants [of the sheriffs] who takes money for carriage, shall take no more from carts and horses than is necessary, and only from carts and horses that are for hire, and not from those

---

[70] 28 Sept. 1356, sheriffs instructed to hold an assize of *novel disseisin* every week, and an assize of *mort d'ancestor* every fortnight, *CLBG*, 72. See *London Possessory Assizes*, ed. H.M. Chew (London Record Society, 1965), pp. xvii–xviii.

[71] These paragraphs as far as the clause about the yeomen of the sheriffs, are copied in French into *Liber Albus*, 46–7.

[72] 28 Sept. 1356, agreed by the mayor, aldermen and an 'immense commonalty', *CLBG*, 74.

belonging to poor people bringing victuals and other merchandise to the city, except for carts and horses that are hired for personal profit, upon pain of losing his office forever.[73]

[Landlord–Tenant Relations][74]

Also everyone who rents any lands or tenements from a denizen or foreigner within the city franchise without a specific contract for a certain term or for life, if that party voluntarily wishes [to terminate the lease], if the rent is less than 40s. per year then he must give the landlord at least three months' notice, and if the rent is more than 40s. per year, then the landlord should have six months' notice.

[f. 154]

And if the tenant fails to give such notice he shall be liable to pay the landlord for the rent of three months, or six months, according to the annual rent charge as above, or he shall find a suitable tenant for the landlord for those terms.

And the landlord shall give the same notice to the tenant whenever he wishes to repossess his own lands and tenements for his own use.

And if the tenant has a special contract by deed for a life interest, or for a specified term, and the landlord sells the lands and tenements, in that case the sale shall not disturb the tenant in the enjoyment of his lease. But if the tenant does not have a special contract by deed, then the purchaser may do as he wishes.

And if the tenant argues that he made a covenant with the landlord exclusively in the presence and hearing of good men, but without a deed, then he shall have an action of covenant against the landlord, and the purchaser shall be free to do as he wishes.

And if the tenant's goods are seized by process at the suit of any person, and the tenant owes money to the landlord for unpaid rent, then the landlord shall be paid his rent before the first plaintiff receives anything. That is to say, if the landlord swears that the tenant is behind with the rent, and provided that the landlord's claim is not greater than for two years' rent; but if he has allowed his tenant to accumulate more than two years' debt, then the remainder is at peril of writ of *mesne* [by which a tenant could recover damages], without prejudice to the claims of other creditors. But if the tenant owes him other debts, the landlord may take action at common law according to the customs and usages of the city.

---

73   2 Apr. 1371, valets of the sergeants of the sheriffs are not to take more carts and horses than necessary, and only from those who hired out carts, *CLBG*, 149. See C.A. Martin, 'Transport for London 1250–1550' (University of London Ph.D. thesis, 2008), 243–7.

74   This section as far as 'according to the customs and usages of the city' is copied in French into *Liber Albus*, 448–9.

[f. 154v]

Also, if anyone rents a house, lands or tenements for a certain term, or for life, and he makes wooden easements [fittings] that are attached to the principal timbers of the tenement by iron nails, of the size of 4*d.* the hundred or larger, or if they are attached by wooden pins or nails by which the principal timber is pierced in part or through, then those easements must remain with the landlord.[75]

And if the tenant makes a hearth, or furnace with lead, or cauldron, or oven of clay or of stone, these shall remain wholly with the landlord.

And the tenant, when he leaves, shall empty the house of all the rubbish he has accumulated within the said house.

But it shall be lawful for the tenant to carry away when he leaves the leads and cauldrons that he has had made there, provided that they have not been fixed or attached within the walls of the house – whether they are made of stone or wood – without the permission of the landlord.

And if a disagreement arises about such fixtures and fittings between the landlord and the tenant, then the ward constables and scavengers, or some of them or, if necessary, some of the city's sworn masons and carpenters, shall judge the dispute in the following way: if the tenant feels himself aggrieved because of faulty roofing or other essential housing necessities with their appendages which the landlord is bound by contract to repair and maintain, and the tenant has warned him, or his rent collector, in the presence of good men who have knowledge of the situation and will bear witness to the faults, which neither the landlord, nor his agent caused to be mended within a month of being warned, then it shall be lawful for the tenant to set the costs of repairs, as supervised by the ward constables and scavengers, against the next rent charge.

[f. 155]

Also all pleaders who plead in city courts shall plead in English, and in no other manner, so that lay people may know the manner of their pleas.[76]

And no pleaders may transfer their days, nor speak for their clients within the bar of the court, unless he is the Common Pleader [Common Sergeant at Law]. But they must remain outside the bar, without making any cry or noise, so that lawyers, and the good men of the city, may

75   The sense, but not the detail, of this provision is found in a decision of 28 Nov. 1365 which was later copied into *Liber Albus*: *CLBG*, 205; *Liber Albus*, 432.

76   28 Sept. 1356, decided that plaintiffs in sheriffs' courts were to plead in English, *CLBG*, 73. In 1362 the use of English in law courts was ordered by statute, *PROME*, v. 152–3.

hear and attend in due manner to their needs and the business that they have to pursue in the courts.[77]

The Charter for the removal and change of aldermen[78]

Edward by the grace of God etc. Know you that among other articles which the Lord Edward, late king of England, our father, in the eleventh year of his reign [1317–18], by his Letters Patent to the citizens of our city of London, for the amelioration and amendment of the same and for the common weal and profit of all the inhabitants and those who dwell in the same city and of those coming there, grants and confirms in the same letters patent that the aldermen of the city, every year, namely on the day of St. Gregory the Pope [12 March], the discharges shall be made by the commonalty of the same city, and they are to be removed for the following year and not to be chosen again, but in the place of those removed others are to be chosen by the same wards from which the aldermen were so removed as is fully contained in the said letters patent.

Upon which, on behalf of the said commonalty, by their petition recently made to us in our Great Council, now newly made to us, meekly prayed and sought that, since there were diverse controversies and opposi-tions between the aldermen and the commonalty of that city, about the removal of aldermen, because of the dishonest and malevolent inter-pretation of words contained in the aforesaid articles,

[f. 155v]

so much arose by the aforesaid aldermen affirming that by those words 'that they should be removed by the commonalty' ought to mean that they should not be removed without certain charges made against the said alderman by the commonalty, or for other notable faults found in the same alderman. But other citizens of the city take the contrary view, so for a long while there has been contention and strife.

We vouchsafe to remove all doubt between them about that article, and command it to be declared more fully and openly.

For in fact we assent to the aforesaid petition more gladly, so that the same mayor, aldermen and the commonalty, may henceforth dwell in tranquillity, rest and peace and abide favourably inclined,

That to the citizens and their successors, by agreement of our Council, we declare the following:

---

[77]   28 Sept. 1356, decided that pleaders and attorneys should remain outside the bar of the sheriffs' court, *CLBG*, 74; reiterated in 1393/4, LBH, f. 286v; also in *Liber Albus*, 521–2.

[78]   See Birch, *Charters*, 65–6, dated 2 Nov. 1376, *CPR 1374–77*, p. 387. In fact the charter of Edward II was dated 8 June 1319, see Birch, *Charters*, 45–50, at p. 46.

That is to say that all and every elected alderman, every year in perpetuity on the feast of St. Gregory the Pope, shall utterly and entirely cease to hold the office of alderman and shall be completely dismissed, and they shall not be eligible for the office of alderman in the following year, but in their place another wise fellow citizen of good unblemished fame shall be elected and chosen by the same wards from which the aldermen have been discharged every year in perpetuity.

In witness whereof we firmly make these our letters patent. Witness myself at Westminster, 22 November, the fiftieth year of our reign of our realm of England, and the thirty-seventh year of the reign in fact of our realm of France [1376].[79]

The Articles for the Regulation of the sale of fish and other victuals in the City of London and elsewhere in our realm of England ordained and established by statute in Parliament held at Westminster the sixth year of his reign [November 1382][80]

[f. 156]

First it is ordained and established by statute that neither in the city of London nor in other cities, boroughs, towns, ports by the sea throughout the aforesaid realm shall any victualler from henceforth have, exercise or occupy any judicial office in any manner, except in those towns where qualified persons may not be found. In this case only, the judge who is standing shall, for the time he is a judge, completely cease and abstain from the practise of victualling on pain of forfeiture of those victuals.

Also it is ordained and agreed that any foreigner or alien who is a friend of the king, coming within the city of London or in other cities, boroughs and towns within the aforesaid realm, whether within the franchise or without, coming with fish and other victuals, whoever he is, may stay there and in future go again with their own goods and they will remain in the safeguard and special protection of our lord the king, and by virtue of this statute it shall be lawful for them from henceforth to sell their fish and aforesaid victuals retail or in gross, without any impediment or objection whatsoever, to cut or trim fish both part and whole, as it pleases them best to sell for their own profit, notwithstanding any charters, ordinances, privileges or customs to the contrary.

Also it is ordained and agreed that anyone who acts as a host both in the city of London and in the great towns of Yarmouth, Scarborough, Winchelsea and Rye and whatever other towns on the sea coast and

---

79   The charter was in fact granted on 2 Nov. 1376, not 22 Nov.: *CPR*, 1374–77, p. 387.
80   Statute passed when John of Northampton was mayor; repealed Nov. 1383 when Nicholas Brembre was mayor, see *CLBH*, 209, 226, See n. 41 above.

elsewhere throughout the realm, both within the liberty and without, from henceforth shall utterly dismiss those that are iniquitous, wrongdoers and forestallers [i.e. interceptors of provisions in order to resell at a higher price], [f. 156v] and the king especially forbids any of these men under peril to act as brokers of herring or other fish or victuals of any kind, or by virtue of any custom, ordinance or privilege or charter previously made to the contrary, which are hereby revoked; and forbids any private or open sale caused or carried out by fishermen, denizens or aliens in the friendship of our lord the king, whereby they, or any one of them at the least, is compelled to sell his fish and victuals, other than where, when and to what and whom they wish, within the aforesaid realm, as he wishes of his own free will.

And moreover it is especially forbidden to every man acting as a host aforesaid that none of them under the aforementioned penalty, henceforth intervene in order to buy or sell or agree to buy or sell, any kind of sea fish or freshwater fish, to the use of any fishmonger or other citizen of the said city of London.

Also likewise, it is forbidden to all fishmongers and citizens of London, that none of them under the same penalty, far or near, from the same city, buy sea fish, fresh fish or freshwater fish from henceforth in order to sell again in the city, except fresh eels, luce and pike, which both denizens and foreigners in common buy, and remain to buy or to sell, as long as the denizens and foreigners within the city are in no way allowed to sell these kinds of fish as often as those fishes are brought or caused to be brought to the aforesaid city.

Also it is ordained that whosoever is mayor of London at the time, among other things, from henceforth shall be charged in his oath that he makes at the exchequer of our lord the king [f. 157] that he will uphold, and cause to be upheld, the ordinance of the fishmongers and victuallers as aforesaid in his bailiwick.

And he shall see that the points of the ordinance are duly performed, and from time to time he shall duly demand that all favours be withdrawn.

And in like manner all mayors, bailiffs and other governors of the cities, boroughs, towns shall be especially charged, pertaining everywhere through all the said realm within the liberty and without, with each and every one of their oaths, upon newly coming into office.

That is to say to cause this ordinance to be held and steadfastly kept as far as they are able in their own bailiwicks.

Charter of Liberties and Franchises granted to the Citizens of London by Henry, the last king of England, 26 March in the fifty-second year of his reign [26 March 1268].[81]

No merchant, or other, is to go to meet merchants coming by land or water with his merchandise and victuals to buy and sell them again until they have come into the city and there set out their merchandise for sale, upon forfeiture of the goods so bought and on pain of imprisonment from which he shall not escape without grievous chastisement.

And no-one is to offer his merchandise for sale until he has paid the custom owing, upon pain of forfeiture of the goods he has brought for sale.

Other articles in the same charter contained, at the instance of the said citizens, we are content to utterly annul for us and our heirs.[82]

---

[81]   For the charter see, Birch, *Charters*, 38–42, at pp. 40–1. Carpenter's summary of royal charters for the city of London includes this charter and also Richard II's fifth charter to the city which includes these two clauses, *Liber Albus*, 138, 155–6.

[82]   This refers to the charter granted to the city by Richard II in 1383, revoking the statute of the previous year, see n. 41, above.

GENERAL INDEX

(excluding the Transcript of Trinity College, Cambridge MS O.3.11, folios 133–157, pp. 47–82)

jurors at   92, 116
meeting days   85
records of   98, 100 and n. 35
inquests
   aldermen and sheriffs excused
      103
   members of common council
      excused   86–7
   suitable men to be returned
      92, 112
London Bridge, wardens   96
mayor   16–17, 18
   choice of sheriff   108
   clerks of   114
   election   87–8 and nn. 8, 10
   escheator   97
   household   94, 100
   oath   39, 42, 89 and n. 12, 124
   seal (signet) of   92, 95
   swordbearer (esquire) of   95
   See also Bamme; Brembre;
      Bury; Cook; Exton;
      Forster; Fraunceys;
      Hadle; Hende; Mordon;
      More; Northampton;
      Pecche; Philpot; Pyel;
      Shaddeworthe; Stable;
      Staundon; Twyford;
      Walworth; Ward;
      Whittington
mayor's court   85, 92–3 and
   n. 17, 99, 116
   bills   93–4
   fees for enrolments   96
   fines   93
mayor's general court   90, 109
rakers, chosen in wardmote   107
recorder   17, 18
   chosen by common council
      99
   duties   92
   election   99 and n. 33
   fee   100
   oath   39, 43, 100 and n. 38
   See also Cheyne; Haldane
records   83, 84 n. 2, 96–7, 98, 109
   keeper of. *See* London,
      civic government,
      chamberlain
   See also London, Letter Books
scavengers   90, 91
   oath   91 and n. 15
   responsible for street cleaning
      91

to be chosen in wardmote
   105, 107, 121
secrecy   17
sergeants of the chamber   85
   chosen by common council
      95
   fees   93
   livery   95 and n. 23
   make arrests   92
   not to brew or bake   114
   number limited to three   95
   oath   99 and n. 32
   See also Wircestre
sergeants of the mayor
   attendance at mayor's court
      92
   fees   93
   number limited to three   95
   oath   99 and n. 32
sheriffs
   counters   91, 114 and n. 65
   duties   87, 113–14, 119
   election   108 and n. 54, 109
      and n. 55
   oath   40, 45, 109 and n. 56
sheriffs' clerks   17, 115, 117
   complaints against   94
   not to brew or bake   114
   oath   39, 111 and n. 59
sheriffs' courts   16, 21, 37, 114–19
   debt cases   117
   not to be held on days of
      common council   85
   records of pleas   109, 114 and
      n. 64
   wager at law   115, 116
   writs of *capias*   115
sheriffs' sergeants
   arrest wrongdoers   92
   attend mayor's court   93
   complaints against   94
   number limited to four   110
      and n. 57, 111
   oath   41, 112 and n. 60
sheriffs' yeomen   111
   complaints against   94
   fees   93
   fees for carriage and carts
      112, 119
   not to brew or bake   114
   oath   113 and n. 61
undersheriff   17, 115
   oath   111

Woodmongers' craft 10, 83.
  See also Asshurst
custumals
  Liber Albus 9, 16–17, 18, 25–6,
    33, 38
  Liber de Ordinacionibus 5, 19
  fire prevention 91, 107–8
  freedom of the City 95, 119
    fees 95, 97
  judicial rights of freemen 114–15,
    118
landlord–tenant relations 120–1
Letter Books
  'D' 11, 16, 33–4, 36, 38
  'G' 10
  'H' 3, 4, 10, 19, 20
places
  Aldersgate 23–4
  Aldgate 23
  Bread Street 114 n. 65
  Cheapside 2
  Guildhall 8, 19, 20, 22, 87–8
  Ludgate 6
  Newgate prison 16, 17
    gaoler 94, 111, 114, 119
    not to be farmed 110, 119
    responsibility of sheriffs 113
  Paternoster Row 28
  Poultry 114 n. 65
  Tower of London, mint 6
  turbulence in 2–3, 25
  wills 94
    executors of 116 and n. 67
Lorimers. *See* London, crafts
Lucas, Margery, wife of Thomas 25
  Thomas, mercer 25
Lyons, Richard, vintner 3

Marchaunt, John, common clerk 22
Masons. *See* London, crafts
Maynard, William, waxchandler 6
Mercers. *See* London, crafts
Merton College, Oxford 22
Middlesex, bailiff 111
  profits belonging to sheriffs 113
  responsibility of sheriffs 109–10
  sheriffs not to farm 119
Mooney, Linne, literary scholar 28
Mordon, Simon de, stockfishmonger,
  mayor 88 n. 11
More, William, vintner, mayor 13
Morton, Robert, gentleman, lawyer 30
Mullesworth (Molesworth),
  Huntingdonshire, manor 29

Multon, John, stationer 28, 30

Northampton, John of, draper, mayor
  6–7, 12, 24
Northbury, Richard, mercer 12

Oaths and oath-taking 11, 15–16, 33–5,
  38
Odyham, Richard, chamberlain
  96 n. 25
Oliver, William, skinner 15
Oresme, Nicholas of 1, 27
  De Moneta 1
Organ, John, mercer 12
Orphans 18, 23–4, 25, 89, 97, 98, 101,
  102, 107

Padyngton, Henry de, common clerk
  96 n. 27
Pahta, Päivi, historical linguist 28
Painters. *See* London, crafts
Parkes, Malcolm, palaeographer 28
Parliament
  1376 ('Good') 3, 23
  1382 102 n. 41, 123 and n. 80,
    125 n. 82
  1383 102 n. 41
  1388 ('Merciless') 8, 10, 26
  1394 101 n. 39
Passelewe, Matthew grocer 14
Paternosterers. *See* London, crafts
Peasants' Revolt (1381) 5, 6, 21
Pecche, John, fishmonger, mayor 3
Pepperers. *See* London, crafts
Perot, Henry, common clerk 22,
  96 n. 27
Philpot, John, grocer, mayor 10, 12
Pouchmakers. *See* London, crafts
Pountfret, John, saddler 15
  William, skinner 15
Prisons. *See* London, civic government,
  sheriffs, counters; London, places,
  Newgate
Pyel, John, mercer, mayor 12
Pykenham, Walter, skinner 15

Reynhout, Lucien, manuscript scholar
  29
Reynold, Richard, mercer 9
Richard II, king of England 25
Roolf, Thomas, skinner 13
Rose, John, skinner 13
Rule, William, draper 15
Rye, Sussex 123–4

LONDON RECORD SOCIETY

President: The Rt. Hon. The Lord Mayor of London

Chairman: Professor Caroline M. Barron, MA, Ph.D., FRHistS
Hon. Secretary: Dr. Helen Bradley
Hon. Treasurer: Dr. David Lewis
Hon. General Editors: Dr. Robin Eagles, Dr. Hannes Kleineke, Professor Jerry White

The London Record Society was founded in December 1964 to publish transcripts, abstracts and lists of the primary sources for the history of London, and generally to stimulate interest in archives relating to London. Membership is open to any individual or institution. Prospective members should apply to the Hon. Membership Secretary, Dr. Penny Tucker, Hewton Farmhouse, Bere Alston, Yelverton, Devon, PL20 7BW (email londonrecordsoc@btinternet.com).

The following volumes have already been published:

12. *The London Eyre of 1276*, edited by Martin Weinbaum (1976)
13. *The Church in London, 1375–1392*, edited by A.K. McHardy (1977)
14. *Committees for the Repeal of the Test and Corporation Acts: Minutes, 1786–90 and 1827–8*, edited by Thomas W. Davis (1978)
15. *Joshua Johnson's Letterbook, 1771–4: Letters from a Merchant in London to his Partners in Maryland*, edited by Jacob M. Price (1979)
16. *London and Middlesex Chantry Certificate, 1548*, edited by C.J. Kitching (1980)
17. *London Politics, 1713–1717: Minutes of a Whig Club, 1714–17*, edited by H. Horwitz; *London Pollbooks, 1713*, edited by W.A. Speck and W.A. Gray (1981)
18. *Parish Fraternity Register: Fraternity of the Holy Trinity and SS. Fabian and Sebastian in the Parish of St. Botolph without Aldersgate*, edited by Patricia Basing (1982)
19. *Trinity House of Deptford: Transactions, 1609–35*, edited by G.G. Harris (1983)
20. *Chamber Accounts of the Sixteenth Century*, edited by Betty R. Masters (1984)
21. *The Letters of John Paige, London Merchant, 1648–58*, edited by George F. Steckley (1984)
22. *A Survey of Documentary Sources for Property Holding in London before the Great Fire*, by Derek Keene and Vanessa Harding (1985)
23. *The Commissions for Building Fifty New Churches*, edited by M.H. Port (1986)
24. *Richard Hutton's Complaints Book*, edited by Timothy V. Hitchcock (1987)
25. *Westminster Abbey Charters, 1066–c.1214*, edited by Emma Mason (1988)
26. *London Viewers and their Certificates, 1508–1558*, edited by Janet S. Loengard (1989)
27. *The Overseas Trade of London: Exchequer Customs Accounts, 1480–1*, edited by H.S. Cobb (1990)
28. *Justice in Eighteenth-Century Hackney: the Justicing Notebook of Henry Norris and the Hackney Petty Sessions Book*, edited by Ruth Paley (1991)
29. *Two Tudor Subsidy Assessment Rolls for the City of London: 1541 and 1582*, edited by R.G. Lang (1993)
30. *London Debating Societies, 1776–1799*, compiled and introduced by Donna T. Andrew (1994)
31. *London Bridge: Selected Accounts and Rentals, 1381–1538*, edited by Vanessa Harding and Laura Wright (1995)
32. *London Consistory Court Depositions, 1586–1611: List and Indexes*, by Loreen L. Giese (1997)
33. *Chelsea Settlement and Bastardy Examinations, 1733–66*, edited by Tim Hitchcock and John Black (1999)
34. *The Church Records of St. Andrew Hubbard Eastcheap, c.1450–c.1570*, edited by Clive Burgess (1999)

Previously published titles in the series are available from Boydell and Brewer; please contact them for further details, or see their website, www.boydellandbrewer.com